Teilhard de Chardin

Makers of the Modern Theological Mind

Bob E. Patterson, Editor

KARL BARTH by *David L. Mueller*
DIETRICH BONHOEFFER by *Dallas M. Roark*
RUDOLF BULTMANN by *Morris Ashcraft*
CHARLES HARTSHORNE by *Alan Gragg*
WOLFHART PANNENBERG by *Don Olive*
TEILHARD DE CHARDIN by *Doran McCarty*
EMIL BRUNNER by *J. Edward Humphrey*
MARTIN BUBER by *Stephen M. Panko*
SÖREN KIERKEGAARD by *Elmer Duncan*

Makers of the Modern Theological Mind

Bob E. Patterson, Editor

TEILHARD DE CHARDIN

by Doran McCarty

Word Books, Publisher, Waco, Texas

Teilhard de Chardin

Library of Congress catalog card number: 75–19911
Printed in the United States of America

To
Professors Dale Moody and Eric Rust
who first introduced me
to Pierre Teilhard de Chardin

Contents

Editor's Preface

Who are the thinkers that have shaped Christian theology in our time? This series tries to answer that question by providing a reliable guide to the ideas of the men who have significantly charted the theological seas of our century. In the current revival of theology, these books will give a new generation the opportunity to be exposed to significant minds. They are not meant, however, to be a substitute for a careful study of the original works of these makers of the modern theological mind.

This series is not for the lazy. Each major theologian is examined carefully and critically—his life, his theological method, his most germinal ideas, his weaknesses as a thinker, his place in the theological spectrum, and his chief contribution to the climate of theology today. The books are written with the assumption that laymen will read them and enter into the theological dialogue that is so necessary to the church as a whole. At the same time they are carefully enough designed to give assurance to a Ph.D. student in theology preparing for his preliminary exams.

Each author in the series is a professional scholar and

theologian in his own right. All are specialists on, and in some cases have studied with, the theologians about whom they write. Welcome to the series.

BOB E. PATTERSON, Editor

Preface

The thought of Pierre Teilhard de Chardin burst upon the world after his death almost without warning, because during his lifetime he was prevented by his superiors in the Roman Catholic church from propagating or printing his ideas. This action against Teilhard caused at least two problems which are reflected in this book. First, the limitation placed on Teilhard hindered him from sharpening his thinking against the emory of reaction to his ideas. Second, he seldom had the need to organize his ideas in relation to the totality about which he was so fond of speaking.

These realities limit any interpreter of Teilhard. This present volume attempts to organize Teilhard's thought in a traditional manner in order to introduce him to the uninitiated reader. But organizing the thought of someone else tends to distort it, especially when the thought of a nonconformist such as Teilhard is forced into traditional patterns of thought.

There are other pitfalls. Teilhard has had many interpreters—some good and some not so good. They have all written in such a relatively short time that the critical sifting of interpretations has not been possible yet. I cannot help but fear that I have followed some of them down a wrong path.

There is one last danger that I recognize. Teilhard's thought has been very stimulating to me personally. His ideas have been seeds for my own thought. As a result, there may be instances when I have not been able to separate Teilhard from McCarty.

Shortly after I began doctoral studies at Southern Baptist Theological Seminary, Professors Dale Moody and Eric Rust introduced me to Pierre Teilhard de Chardin. While I owe them many intellectual, professional and personal debts, it is for this special indebtedness that I have dedicated the book to them.

Several chapters in this volume have evolved out of other papers. One paper was presented to the Faculty Club at Midwestern Baptist Theological Seminary. Another was my convocation address at Midwestern.

I am grateful to my colleague, Morris Ashcraft, for suggesting my name to Bob Patterson in connection with this volume. I thank Bob Patterson, a friend since seminary days, for asking me to write the book. I appreciate the graciousness of my friends, Mr. and Mrs. Earl Atlakson, for the use of their vacation house in the beautiful woods near St. Joseph, Missouri, where I was able to put my materials into shape.

To my wife Gloria are due many thanks for her patience, interest and forbearance while this book was in gestation and birth. Also, I owe great thanks to Mrs. Shirley Mynatt, my secretary, for her work typing the manuscript. And I thank my daughter Gaye for reading the manuscript and suggesting stylistic improvements.

DORAN McCARTY

I. Teilhard the Man

In his novel, *The Shoes of the Fisherman*, Morris West wrote:

> The home-coming of Jean Telemond, S.J., was a drab little affair that belied the warmth of his superior's welcome.
> For twenty years he had worked as a paleontologist, in China, in Africa, in America, and the far Indies, plotting the geography of change, the history of life recorded in the crust of the earth. The best scientific minds had been his colleagues and coworkers. He had survived war and revolution and disease and loneliness. He had endured the perilous dichotomy between his function as a scientist and his life as a religious priest. To what end? [1]

West answered his question some pages later when he wrote about the report which a special commission gave to the Pope about Telemond:

> 'The most Reverend Fathers have not desired to take, letter for letter, what the author has written on these points; for otherwise they would be forced to consider some of the author's conclusions as a true and real heresy. They are very well aware of the semantic difficulties involved in expressing a new and original thought, and they wish to concede that the thought of the author may still remain in a problematic phase.'
> 'It is, however, their considered opinion that the Reverend Father Jean Telemond be required to reexamine this work,

15

and those later ones which may depend on it, to bring them into conformity with the traditional doctrine of the Church. In the meantime he should be prohibited from preaching, teaching, publishing, or disseminating in any other fashion the dubious opinions noted by the Fathers of the Sacred Congregation.' [2]

The character whom West calls Telemond is the fictional counterpart of Teilhard. I have been told by a man who spoke to Teilhard's niece that the portrayal by West is true to Teilhard's life in nearly every detail.

TEILHARD'S LIFE

Marie Josef Pierre Teilhard de Chardin came from a patrician family who lived in romantic surroundings. He was born May 1, 1881, in the family chateau of Sarcenat in the ancient province of Auvergne. The province was named after the Gaulish tribe of Arverni whose rule of the area was already established in the days of Julius Caesar. The chateau Sarcenat had been built during the reign of Louis XIII (1610–1643) on high ground above the village of Orcines and about four miles from Clermont-Ferrand. It was acquired by Teilhard's ancestors in 1820. The Teilhard family spent the cold winter months of January to March with their cousins in Clermont.

Teilhard was the family name until 1841 when Pierre's grandfather, Pierre Cirice Teilhard, married Marguerite Victoire Barron de Chardin. Since that time the family name has been Teilhard de Chardin. The son of Pierre Cirice and Marguerite Victoire was Emmanuel. He married Berthe Adile de Dompierre d'Hornoy who was a great grandniece of Voltaire.

Berthe and Emmanuel had eleven children but all did not survive childhood. Pierre was the fourth son, the only one to become a priest. His brothers entered careers in business, engineering, the army and navy. His favorite sister was

Marguerite Marie who, although she was an invalid, became a "Little Sister of the Poor" and a leader in the Catholic Union of the Sick.

Emmanuel Teilhard de Chardin, Pierre's father, was a man of scholarly pursuits, and he personally taught his children Latin until they went off to boarding school. Pierre began his formal school work in 1892 at the Jesuit school of Notre Dame de Mongré, near Lyons, where he was a boarder. Here he began to be interested in philosophy. At sixteen he became aware of a call to be a priest. In 1899, when he was eighteen, he began his Jesuit novitiate at Aix-en-Provence in southern France. From there he went north to the school at Laval to study further for the priesthood. At Laval on March 25, 1901, he took his first vows.

This was a time of much feeling against the church, and in 1901 anticlericalism in France reached its highest point with the political policy called *Lois d'exception*. The passage of this act, aimed against the religious orders of the church, prompted the Jesuits at Laval to transfer the school to the English island of Jersey a short way off the French coast. Teachers and students, including Teilhard, traveled in civilian costumes complete with top hats and motoring capes.

The period at Jersey provided a creative stimulus for Teilhard's study of nature, which had been his passion all through his schooling. He had already been introduced to geology and palaeontology, for the area of Auvergne in central France where he had been raised offered abundant resources for these subjects. Jersey offered him new terrain to study with different types of rocks and fossils to discover. In addition there were the abundant lessons to be learned from the marine life washed up on the beaches.

In 1905, when he was twenty-four, Teilhard was sent to Cairo to teach in the Jesuits' secondary school. A three-year period of teaching was part of the Jesuit's training for the priesthood. There he was put in charge of the museum which he found to be a jumble of assembled material rather than a systematic collection. His assignment was to teach chemistry and physics, even though he had not prepared himself to teach either subject. Teilhard did not find his years in Egypt boring, since they gave him the opportunity of examining the many evidences and artifacts of Egypt's ancient history. His letters to his parents show that he found time to study the plant life about him, and to hunt for fossils. He sent some of his fossil finds to Paris to members of the Geological Society, and was gratified to have a new species of fossil fish named after him.

After his three years in Egypt, Teilhard returned for his four years of theological study to the Jesuit school at Hastings, England. This was the period when Pope Pius X was attacking modernism in theology. But while Teilhard took his theological studies seriously, he did not share the desire for bitter theological jousting which was prevalent. On August 24, 1911, Teilhard was ordained to the priesthood. His final vows were not taken until May 1918, just before the end of World War I.

One of the most significant events for Teilhard at Hastings was not theological but palaeontological. He had the opportunity to meet Charles Dawson, the famous palaeontologist, and Professor Sir Arthur Woodward, head of the palaeontological department of the British Museum. He even did some digging with them, and unearthed an elephant molar. This was on the site where Dawson "found" the skull of the Piltdown Man (Eoanthropus) which later was proved to be a hoax. It is unfortunate that this was Teilhard's first exposure to palaeontological drama.

In the autumn of 1912, Teilhard was assigned by his Jesuit superiors to pursue his scientific research at the Institut de Paléontologie, which was a part of Musée d'Histoire naturelle (Museum of Natural History) in Paris.

During his studies, which continued until 1914, he made trips to important palaeontological sites, examining prehistoric paintings, mines, rock formations of mountain ranges. He also paid another visit to the site of the Piltdown Man. It was during this period that he became associated with the master professor of palaeontology at the Paris museum, Marcellin Boule. Through Boule Teilhard met many who would be his co-workers throughout his life.

One of the long interludes of Teilhard's life came about because of the First World War. Teilhard sought a position as an ambulance driver but was turned down. Instead he served as a stretcher-bearer with a North African regiment from 1914 to 1919. In this capacity he had many opportunities to act as a priest for the wounded and dying, offering them his warm care, as well as prayers and the celebration of the Mass. At one point during the war he was offered the position of chaplain, but turned it down saying, "I am of more use in the ranks; I can do more good there." Already he was showing the kind of positive and hopeful attitude, even in the midst of war, which would mark his life with its most distinctive characteristic. As a result of his service in the war, he received the Médaille Militaire, and on May 21, 1921, at the request of his old regiment, he was made a Chevalier of the Legion d'Honneur.

After his army duties Teilhard did doctoral studies at the Sorbonne and in 1922 successfully defended his doctoral dissertation on palaeontological discoveries of the Lower Eocene period in France, receiving the title of doctor with distinction. Part of his research was done with pickax in hand alongside the peasants working in an archaeological site near Rheims.

During this time he also taught geology at the Institut Catholique in Paris. Apparently his belief in evolution had been a growing conviction since his days at Hastings, and his advocacy of evolution at the Institut brought him into conflict with his religious superiors. They had expected him to quash the theories of Darwin in his teaching. Although Teilhard did oppose the straight evolution of Darwin, he clearly advocated transformism, that is, an evolution of

gradual transformation. Teilhard was the further object of
suspicion because of close associates who suffered censure
from Merry du Val, the powerful secretary of the Holy
Office in Rome. One of the most damaging and decisive
points was the trivial incident where a young theologian en-
gaged Teilhard in a discussion. Teilhard obliged the young
man by writing down a couple of pages of notes on original
sin. These were read not only by the young man but by those
who sought to cause Teilhard difficulty. The eventual result
of the conflict was that Teilhard was forbidden to teach at the
Institut, though this did not happen until after his first period
of time in China.

While he was teaching at the Institut, a box of fossils came
to the museum from a fellow Jesuit geologist, Père Emile
Licent, in Tientsin, on the north coast of China. Teilhard was
given the task of classifying them. This led to a correspond-
ence with Licent, and then to an invitation to join Licent and
his work in China. Many men have talked about superiors
sending them to Outer Mongolia as a figure of speech, but
Teilhard literally ended up in the Ordos Desert in Inner
Mongolia. The center of his activities, however, was Tientsin,
where Licent had a museum.

Teilhard considered France his home and the center of
his world, and returned to Paris in 1924, when he taught
again at the Institut Catholique. But then the word forbidding
his teaching came through and he was ordered back to China.
The Institut kept his name on their books as a teacher in
absence, but after a year they were forced to remove his
name altogether. In 1927, on his next visit to France, the
doors were no more open and he was no more officially
welcome, though his associates at the Institut were already
circulating typescripts of his writings. The exile from France
caused him great pain, but he never allowed himself to become bitter and was able to say that all things that happen are
matters of adoration.

His third trip to China included brief expeditions into

French Somaliland and Ethiopia. During this period he also
went on some extended research expeditions in China itself.
Because the trips were to remote spots they were arduous
and dangerous. Once he wrote in a letter:

> Our journey ended happily enough, but there was some diffi-
> culty between Jehol and the Great Wall. The country was full
> of bandits ('big' bandits this time) and we were only able to
> cross the last cols in the wake of a military convoy we
> providentially met. And we took care not to lag behind.[3]

It was in this third period in China that Teilhard participated in his most celebrated palaeontological field research—
the discovery of the Peking Man, Sinanthropus, which was
found at Chou-kou-Tien. While the magnitude of the importance of Chou-kou-Tien would only be evident later, Teilhard
predicted its value when he described how he became involved
with the work in his letter of May 6, 1929:

> A letter from Ting urgently begged me to get down to
> Chou-Kou-Tien, 30 miles south of Peking, to study with two
> Chinese the geology of the site and supervise the organisation
> of the year's new excavations. To take charge of Chou-Kou-
> Tien is too important a job for me to think of refusing. So I
> started back for the capital with my camp-bed and some
> provisions. A little Ford took me and my two companions
> over impossibly bad roads to a village near the dig.[4]

While it was a worker, Pei Wen Chung, who first discovered the Peking Man, it was Teilhard's palaeontological
interpretation of the remains of this prehistoric creature
which was crucial and decisive. Teilhard was the geologist
at Chou-kou-Tien at the time of the discovery and he later
became director of the project.

One of the things which influenced the Chinese to ask
Teilhard to help was his sympathetic attitude toward their
emerging sense of nationalism. The policy of many foreign
scientists was that of exploitation of ancient Chinese artifacts,
many of which ended up in museums out of China. When the

Chinese tried to keep important artifacts in China, they found a friend in Teilhard.

Teilhard returned to France in 1930 and made a special visit to his family, especially to see his ailing father, who died in 1932 during his next period in China. On this visit he was persuaded to make his first trip to the United States and lecture for the Osburn Research Club and Columbia University in New York City, where he made a number of new friends. He continued on to China by way of San Francisco.

The most important project in which Teilhard was involved when he returned to China in 1931 was an expedition that became known as the Croisière Jaune—the Yellow Expedition—sponsored by Citroen to demonstrate that their half-track caterpillar vehicles could traverse the heart of central Asia, which is primarily desert. Teilhard was invited to participate as the official geologist. Half the group, including Teilhard, started from Peking, crossed the Gobi Desert, and ended in Aksu in Sinkiang. The other half started from Beirut and crossed the Himalayas.

The project gained great publicity because of its dramatic nature—a dangerous trip across relatively unknown and uncharted country, with threats to the expedition's safety from local kings and their armies. The east-west group was held prisoner for two months in Urumchi by the ruler of Sinkiang—that area northwest of China proper and north of Tibet that Teilhard described as the most impenetrable frontier in the world.

All across the Gobi Desert Teilhard had the opportunity of seeing geological formations which helped him form his ideas about the nature of the earth, and of doing geological research where few geologists (if any) had ever been able to work. When he could, he made collection of significant material, though he was hampered from doing the concentrated type of research familiar to geologists, since he could only collect specimens when the vehicles were being repaired or a brief respite was being taken for the personnel. But he could observe the formations as they drove by, and he recorded his observations and impressions. In the following paragraph he summarized his first few weeks:

> Since the 12th of May we have already covered 500 miles of this wonderful Mongolian country: on the second day a snowstorm, on the third a sandstorm, and now beautiful weather. In these few days I have already gathered a considerable store of geological data really *'illuminating'* for the structure of the Gobi, which is encouraging for the future. The type of quick research that I was envisaging turns out to be both possible and rewarding; and on top of that it has been pleasant going. This vast oceanlike expanse, furrowed by sharp ridges of rock, inhabited by gazelles, dotted with white and red lamaseries, and trodden by Mongols in clothes as filthy as they are colourful, is extremely 'taking'; the more so perhaps that being obliged to get to understand it, I am settling down as though I were quite at home. My companions, too, are delightful.[5]

Following the completion of the Croisière Jaune, Teilhard returned to Peking, making his headquarters there. In the next few years, prior to World War II, there were brief visits to France and the United States, as well as geological and palaeontological expeditions to India, Java and Burma, all of which greatly excited him and increased his scientific knowledge of prehistoric man.

The longest single period of his exile in China began in 1939 and lasted until 1946. The Japanese war, first with China and then with the Allies, made it impossible for him to leave during this period. Although the conditions were often not the best, he was able to continue his work. He was separated from easy access to Père Licent's museum and had to do much of his work in his home. Social activities were curtailed by travel restrictions and curfews.

With the ending of the war, Teilhard's exile in China was over. He returned to Paris and made his home there from 1946 to 1951· Although he was not in good health (he suf-

fered a heart attack in June 1947), he continued to write, and
was able to travel and lecture occasionally. He was promoted
to Officer in the Legion d'Honneur "for outstanding services
to the intellectual and scientific influence of France. . . . He
may now be regarded, in the field of palaeontology and geology, as one of the chief ornaments of French science. . . ."

In 1948 Teilhard visited Rome with the hope of accom-
plishing two things. He had been approached about accepting
a professorship at the Collège de France in Paris, and he
wanted to have the ban on his teaching activity lifted. Also he
wanted to get the official Roman Catholic approval, the imprimatur, on one or more of his writings. While he never got
to speak to the Pope, he carried his appeals as far as possible.
The answer he received was that he should not allow any
further consideration of his name for the professorship at the
Collège de France. While he was not immediately informed,
he was not granted the imprimatur.

Teilhard began a new and, as it turned out, the final period
of his life in 1951 with a new exile—this time in the United
States. The Wenner Gren Foundation funded Teilhard for
lectures and an expedition, and finally asked him to be a re-
search associate. During his last years, he made two trips to
South Africa to learn about palaeontological research there.
He also made one last visit to France and to his home at
Sarcenat.

Pierre Teilhard de Chardin died on Easter Sunday, April
11, 1955, in New York City. He was laid in his final resting
place in upper New York the following Wednesday.*

TEILHARD'S RELIGION

Teilhard's faith was marked by a simplicity of practice and a
serenity which was characteristic of his whole life. His theory
of faith, however, was very complex, and around it brewed

---

* For a chronology of events in Teilhard's life, see the Appendix.

both personal and confessional storms. Harsh and sometimes official accusations were made against Teilhard in regard to his orthodoxy, church faithfulness, and even his Christianity. By 1924 he had clashed with his superiors, with the result that he was forbidden to take a teaching post in Paris because of the way he expressed his ideas about original sin and evolution. He was forced to subscribe to six propositions of which only one really caused him difficulty.

Upon the request of Msgr. Bruno de Solages, Teilhard wrote a paper which has been published under the title *How I Believe*.[6] Although it was written in 1934, it remained unpublished (as did the rest of his work) until after his death. Here he spoke of his belief in terms of three faiths:

> Faith in the unity of the world, faith in the existence and faith in the immortality of the spirit which is born from the synthesis of the world—these three faiths, summed up in the worship of a personal and personalizing center of universal convergence—these, let me say once more, are the terms of that creed.[7]

Teilhard understood that his faith was the result of an evolution. One way to talk about the evolution of faith is to see the historical progress and formation of one's own religious life. An important part of Teilhard's religious life were the roots he put down in his childhood along with his family. Teilhard's family had been deep in the service of the church for several generations. His parents were practicing Christians, for whom prayer and attendance at daily mass were a way of life. His mother has been described as a model of piety. It was this early training that helped Teilhard through the stormy seas so that he did not go under the waves of cynicism or apostasy.

Another element in Teilhard's faith came from his nationality. There was a special kind of spirit among French Catholics which sometimes took on the arrogance of zeal. The persecution of the church that came during Teilhard's Jesuit training surely reinforced the deep sense of commitment toward the church which had already been implanted in him during his childhood experiences. Ironically, this same French Catholic zeal and enthusiasm manifested itself in the rigid interpretation of Catholic dogma that led to his superiors' rejection of Teilhard's thought. Late in his life, he was even barred from visiting Paris, although he finally received permission to do so in 1954.

Above all Teilhard was a Roman Catholic. As a member of the Jesuit Order he attempted to live obediently, from his own perspective, to his vows. He refused to leave the church when he was denied the imprimatur. He also refused to publish without it. He sought the favor of the officials of the church in order to publish, and when refused, he attempted to show in private that his ideas were acceptable rather than make public attacks. Abbé Paul Grenet described him as "an obedient but stubborn son of the church." [8] He probably would have suffered less by publishing without the imprimatur than by writing as he did—without the benefit of publication.

Many of Teilhard's critics believe that his religious loyalties should have been only with the Roman Catholic Church. However, Teilhard realized that such a restriction would be a denial of his entire philosophical system. No term has been coined which is adequate to describe this wider religion of Teilhard. *Ecumenism* is inadequate, because the word usually refers to the crossing of denominational lines within Christianity. Teilhard's religion was not a kind of Bahai religion, because he had a critical, less naïve assessment of the religions of the world. This aspect of Teilhard has often been called (accusingly) *universalism*. While the criticism has some validity, his universalism would have to be defined differently from the usual definition.

The cosmic scope of Teilhard's thought broadened his understanding of the role of religion. For him religion was "born of the earth's need for the disclosing of a god." [9] His belief was that Christ was not just a historical person, Jesus of Nazareth, but that he is the whole inner energy of the universe and the goal to which all of the universe is moving. Out of this kind of perspective he could write a "Hymn to the Universe." Christ is not the sole possession of the Christian church but a part of the structure of every man's existence.

During his long exile in the Orient, Teilhard faced another definition of his Christian faith and his religion. Now he was not a Christian because he was a European or a Frenchman. Instead he had to find his religion not over against atheism or secularism but over against the traditional Oriental religions (and later Marxism).

He could not accept the appeal of the Eastern religions, because to them *"matter is dead weight and illusion."* For Teilhard *"matter is heavily loaded, throughout, with sublime potentialities."* He believed that such a view of matter led to the renunciation of the modern world and man's work, whereas the God he sought would be the "saviour of man's work." [10] The mysticism of these religions appealed to Teilhard but he finally had to reject them.

The second kind of religion which Teilhard saw was humanism. Apart from Marxism, humanism had not become an organized religion, but it nevertheless was powerful and had a great appeal. Humanists usually gave a sense of progress in the world with which Teilhard could identify. He said of himself, "By nature and profession I am . . . too much a child of the world not to feel at home in a temple built to the glory of the earth." [11] However, humanistic systems were unsatisfactory for Teilhard because they denied that the spirit was endowed with immortality and personality. Such efforts to build up the body of their religion without reference to those things soon produced the feeling of insecurity, incompleteness and suffocation.

Therefore, as Teilhard put it, "by a process of elimination" Christianity is seen as the eminent religion. The God of Christianity acts in the same way as the person does and "the universe of Christianity culminates in immortal souls, eternally responsible for their own destiny." [12]

Father Teilhard de Chardin did not exclude from Christianity any one who expressly or implicitly believes in Love. He knew that the hour is not the same for every man to realize the Essential Love, cause and purpose of the Universe.[13]

Love is at the very heart of the universe and experienced by every man and is also the spring from which every religion begins. While the three currents (Eastern, humanism and Christian) presently appear to be at cross purposes, they will form one great river someday.

TEILHARD'S FAITH

There exists no unanimous usage of the word *faith*. Teilhard's definition is: "I mean by 'faith' any adherence of our intelligence to a general view of the universe." [14] He also talks about the "evolution of faith." For him, faith is not an analytical exercise but a synthesis of all previously held beliefs, and if those previously held beliefs are incapable of the synthesis, then they are spurious or misunderstood. This was one of the reasons why Teilhard did not see that he was contradicting the Roman church but thought that he was helping by adding an ingredient for the synthesis into the whole or general concept of the universe. Teilhard's thought is that there is no way to have this general view of the whole universe without understanding the place of God in the universe.

Teilhard's Evolution of Faith: The World

I believe that the universe is an evolution.
I believe that the evolution proceeds toward a spirit.
I believe that spirit is fully realized in a form of personality.
I believe that the supremely personal is the universal Christ.[15]

This creed with which Teilhard begins his book *How I Believe* shows us the first step in the evolution of Teilhard's basic faith. It is faith in the world. Why is faith in the world basic? The world contains the basic building blocks for life physically and spiritually. The youngest child is smothered with an infinite number of images of the world in which he lives, but the child does not stop with these multiple perceptions. The child begins to make "sense" out of them by seeing that all of the perceptions and images form a world. This is the transition from an ensemble to a whole, just as there is the transformation of some bright dots on a page called a musical score into an anthem.

There are two possible approaches according to Teilhard —that of the pluralist and that of the monist. The monist attempts to see the whole behind the many objects of perception and experiences, sensing that there *is* something behind all of the parts. That is faith in the world rather than a skepticism based on particles. The pluralist identifies the many parts and experiences without admitting that they form a purposeful pattern. Teilhard was a monist.

Teilhard's Evolution of Faith: The Spirit

The next stage of faith is faith in the spirit. Teilhard points out that the materialists are working with an illusion. Earlier scientists and materialists had washed away the "spirit in floods of material particles. Spirit no longer existed—there was nothing but matter." He believed that this retrogression had changed and now the converse concepts were rising again. No doubt, he was partially referring to the rise of quantum physics. At any rate he said "matter no longer exists, there is nothing but spirit." [16] Taken out of context that may very well seem like a kind of Gnosticism, which Teilhard did not intend. Like Henri Bergson, he saw spirit as the primary quality or interiorization while matter is the externalization of spirit. Spirit is the dynamic "withinness" while matter is the "without." (We will discuss this further in chap. II.)

Teilhard's Evolution of Faith: Immortality

Teilhard also had faith in immortality. If spirit is act and is not the static stuff we normally think of as matter, then is spirit significant? Teilhard's answer is yes. Spirit is that psyche which lasts through all of the different forms of matter and the historical exigencies. Previously it had been thought that things were held together from below by the external which we call matter. However Teilhard saw this as an inversion of reality, because things are really held together from above by spirit. It is the unseen energy which accounts for life and reality. Without that energy matter would be dead, lifeless, and disappear. His argument runs like this:

> And, indeed, if the world, taken as one whole, is something infallible (first stage); and if, moreover, it moves toward spirit (second stage); then, it must be capable of providing us with what is essentially necessary to the continuation of such a movement. By this I mean it must provide *ahead of us an unlimited* horizon. Without this, the world would be incapable of sustaining the progress it stimulates, and would be in the inadmissible situation of having to wither away in apathy every time the consciousness born in it reached the age of reason.[17]

Teilhard's Evolution of Faith: Personality

The last stage in Teilhard's evolution of faith is his faith in personality. He points out that a monist usually describes the universe's ultimate spirit as an impersonal force in which our personalities will be engulfed. Teilhard defends the idea that every living being must culminate in a personal being in which we are to be *superpersonalized.* It is not something about a man that survives, but it is the growth center of a man —his psyche or his real person—which survives. That is what he calls personality.

THE SPIRITUALITY OF TEILHARD

If we look at Teilhard as a scientist only, we miss an important ingredient in his whole work—a call for a renewal in spirituality. Spirituality for Teilhard was the road to personalization, which in turn was the highest achievement.

Teilhard's first major work was not scientific but spiritual —*Le Milieu Divin*. This work is often difficult for readers to comprehend because the reader anticipates some kind of intellectualized world view. It is rather the verbalized reflection of Teilhard's own spirituality which had been lived and a sort of spiritual exercise of mystic tradition. Indeed it has been compared to Saint Ignatius's *Spiritual Exercises.*

Even so, Teilhard recognized that his beginning point of faith was not the result of such spiritual exercises but the reaction to God's grace when it confronted him. "I have the impression that the birth of my faith was an almost organic phenomenon, almost a reflex, like the eyes' response to light." [18] His faith was not a learned exercise but an intuitive, spontaneous experience where relationships beyond words suddenly make sense.

Teilhard explained his spiritual attitude once in a letter:

> The longer I live, the more I feel that true repose consists in 'renouncing' one's own self, by which I mean making up one's mind to admit that there is no importance whatever in being 'happy' or 'unhappy' in the usual meaning of the words. Personal success or personal satisfaction are not worth another thought if one does achieve them, or worth worrying about if they evade one or are slow in coming. All that is really worth while is action—faithful action, for the world, and in God. Before one can see that and live by it, there is a sort of threshold to cross, or a reversal to be made in what appears to be men's general habit of thought; but once that gesture has been made, what freedom is yours, freedom to work and to love! I have told you more than once that my life is now possessed by this 'disinterest' which I feel to be growing on me, while at the same time the deep-seated appetite, that calls me to all that is real at the heart of the real, continues to grow stronger.[19]

This is not the image of a panting mystic running hard in the pursuit of holiness. It is the spiritual realism of a pilgrim in a hostile environment following his vision of Divine duty.

This type of spirituality is not withdrawal from the world

as has been true in so many manifestations of holiness within
the Roman church. The Roman church has seen excesses akin
to Gnosticism and Manichaeism in which there is denial of all
that is earthly and material. Claude Cuenot points out the
soundness of the theological foundation of Teilhard's spirituality:

> At the root of this spirituality—and this is why it is
> modern—we find a certain concept of divine creation. It has
> no room for the oversimplified idea of a creator God who,
> in the beginning, created the cosmos once and for all, and,
> as it were extrinsically, like a potter shaping a vessel of clay.
> His creative effort is immanent in the world, and the act by
> which he maintains it in being is identical with the creative
> act.[20]

Teilhard's spirituality can be seen by examining his published letters. Many of them are more devotional exercises
than personal communication. Other than *The Divine Milieu*,
the work which is the most consciously oriented toward spirituality is *Hymn of the Universe*. Poetic passages merging
science, philosophy, and theology into spirituality are evident throughout this book. Here is one striking passage:

> Over every living thing which is to spring up, to grow, to
> flower, to ripen during this day say again the words: This is
> my Body. And over every death-force which waits in readi-
> ness to corrode, to wither, to cut down, speak again your com-
> manding words which express the supreme mystery of faith:
> This is my Blood.[21]

While there are times that Henri de Lubac exaggerates the
emphasis of Teilhard (especially Teilhard's adoration of the
Virgin Mary), he nevertheless gives insights into parts of
Teilhard that are often obscured by the scientific and philosophical language of Teilhard's writings. De Lubac calls
special attention to Teilhard's annual retreats. These are
required of all Jesuits. Teilhard always tried to arrange his so
that they would fall on the first days of autumn. Jesuits gen-

erally used the retreats for contemplation of positive spiritual exercises. But Teilhard often used them for personal self-examination. Teilhard was not an intellectual who left spirituality to other priests. He, too, participated in spiritual exercises which stimulated his own spiritual development.

Teilhard's spirituality was yoked to his emphasis upon love which he often referred to with a capital L. Love was not just sentimentality but it was the name for God, the substance of the world, therefore the object of all meditation.

Teilhard was especially sensitive to the Divine presence. Inasmuch as he saw that Spirit was the inner reality of all that we experience, he has been accused of a kind of pantheism. While that accusation cannot be dealt with here, it was the awareness of the presence of God in every particle of the universe which made Teilhard such a sensitive soul. Associated with that Divine presence was prayer. While there were verbal, ritual and ceremonial prayers, Teilhard also saw that every moment was a communion of prayer with the inner being of the world and therefore with the Spirit.

TEILHARD, THE PRIEST

Teilhard did not take his ordination or the Jesuit Order lightly. His letters and memoirs speak eloquently about his excitement at the moment he took his vows. While he was well known for his training as a palaeontologist, it should never be forgotten that his primary training was that of a priest.

When World War I broke out in Europe, Teilhard became a stretcher bearer in the French army, but he never forgot that his primary duty was to God. He saw himself becoming more and more a chaplain. Indeed, he offered communion to those in the trenches. He did not attempt to escape his priestly call but found ways to fulfill it even when he had a nonpriestly assignment.

During Teilhard's exile in China, he ended up in Mongolia on geological expeditions. As was his custom, he kept a diary during those expeditions. They are marked by references to the spiritual condition of the people he found there, references to his own prayers, the saying of the rosary and holding mass. Although he was exiled from Paris, he had not been exiled from his priesthood. Teilhard's faith and his priesthood were inextricably intertwined.

TEILHARD'S MYSTICISM

Mysticism has a rich history in Roman Catholic tradition. Teilhard was an heir and practitioner of the mystical tradition. His mysticism, however, was different from that of many of his predecessors. He did not retreat into a monastery for private ecstasy. Although he was quiet and appeared to be shy, he never cloistered himself away from people. Neither was he the typical mystic who denounced the material world and all of the beauty in it, as did Bernard of Clairvaux. His mysticism and contemplation was through matter to the Spirit rather than the denial of matter in order to elevate the Spirit.

Many of Teilhard's writings are directly mystical or point toward mysticism. Many of his letters were written out of his spiritual hunger to communicate with his close friends in Europe. As a result he not only recounted his experiences, but expressed his deepest feelings and thoughts. We probably would not have these accounts had he not been exiled to the Orient.

Teilhard's most intense mystical writing is *Hymn of the Universe,* a compilation of meditations written at various times in his life, offering contemplations on elements of the universe, matter, communion and Christ.

Some interpreters have not taken Teilhard seriously as a theologian, philosopher or a scientist, and have called him only a mystic. He *was* a mystic and much of his science, theology and philosophy he put in mystical terms. Regardless of how his interpreters count that as a weakness, Teilhard counted it as a strength, because through it he attempted to synthesize the elements of the universe and human and divine experience. He did not see that synthesis as unscientific but as necessary scientifically, since science deals with reality and the inner side of the universe according to Teilhard was as real as the external universe. He believed that to leave out the inner side would be unscientific.

As an example of Teilhard's mystical literature, one can look at *The Mass on the World,* which is included in *Hymn of the Universe.* The titles within that are: The Offering, Fire Over the Earth, Fire in the Earth, Communion, and Prayer. Here is one excerpt typical of his mysticism:

> In the new humanity which is begotten today the Word prolongs the unending act of his own birth; and by virtue of his immersion in the world's womb the great waters of the kingdom of matter have, without even a ripple, been endued with life. No visible tremor marks this inexpressible transformation; and yet, mysteriously and in very truth, at the touch of the supersubstantial Word the immense host which is the universe is made flesh. Through your own incarnation, my God, all matter is henceforth incarnate.[22]

Teilhard did not see science and mysticism as antithetical. In fact he entitled one essay, "The Mysticism of Science," [23] predicting that the hostilities and conflict between science and religion will end in a higher synthesis of the two.

Teilhard was a very complex man, although the complexity was often obscured by his easy and simple manners. He was the confluence of family piety, church loyalty, *avant garde* intellectualism, field researcher, and loyal friend.

II. The Structure of Reality*

Teilhard deals with reality as both a scientist and a philosopher would. As a scientist he describes the makeup of entities which are measurable, something of their effect on each other, and how they build up when allowed to interact. As a philosopher he goes beyond this and attempts to show that there is reality which cannot be measured. He does not excuse the scientist from dealing with the immeasurable, as is so often done when people wish to delineate between science on the one hand and philosophy or religion on the other. Instead he sees that a scientist makes a construct of reality and by eliminating the immeasurable is either correct or incorrect. According to Teilhard, however, the scientist has failed in his job as an observer. He will not excuse the scientist by allowing him to hide behind the curtain of empirical data only, even though this runs the risk of making science more a metaphysics or perhaps a meta-science rather than natural science. Science has been historically tied to primary empirical data only, but if Teilhard had his way, science would no longer accept this voluntary poverty.

---

* A glossary is provided at the end of the book. It is particularly necessary because of Teilhard's use of technical terms, new usages of terms and his creation of new terminology.

MATTER

One would expect a man with the mystical tendencies of Teilhard to be absorbed in the glorification of spirituality and not matter. This expectation is intensified when one realizes that Teilhard spent more than half his adult life in the Orient where there is such strong emphasis on transcendentalism and escapism. However, such a conclusion does not apply to Teilhard. He does have much to say about the spiritual nature of the universe and the ultimate reality which is more psychic than materialistic. For Teilhard, however, matter is the building block of spirituality as well as of the physical universe. He makes no apologies for his appreciation of matter. Nowhere is this more obvious than in a section of his book, *Hymn of the Universe,* which he calls "Hymn to Matter." A part of this hymn is as follows:

> 'Blessed be you, perilous matter, violent sea, untameable passion: you who unless we fetter you will devour us.
> 'Blessed be you, mighty matter, irresistible march of evolution, reality ever new-born; you who, by constantly shattering our mental categories, force us to go ever further and further in our pursuit of the truth. . . .
> 'I acclaim you as the divine *milieu,* charged with creative power, as the ocean stirred by the Spirit, as the clay moulded and infused with life by the incarnate Word.'[1]

It is obvious that Teilhard was no Manichean, and if there is any justification for calling him a Gnostic, such an accusation would certainly have to be qualified. Even if Teilhard believed that the ultimate is spiritual, he was a materialist.

Plurality

Three concepts must be brought into a discussion of Teilhard's idea of matter: plurality, unity, and energy. Teilhard says that there is a substratum of small particles scattered throughout the universe. These small particles make up the basic stuff of the universe. By the word *plurality* which Teilhard uses to describe these particles, he means that they are reduplicated in massive numbers throughout the universe. All of these particles are identical. It would not matter if one particle came from the earth and another from thousands of light years away—they would be the same.

Unity

While these particles form a substratum throughout the universe and are individuated, they also form a unity. It is not possible to say that one particle is here and completely isolated from another particle that is over there. While a particle's sphere of influence may be greater at one point than another, it is coextensive with the entire universe. This of course demands a nonsimplistic view of the time-space dimension, and Teilhard accepts a somewhat Einsteinian view of time-space. The unity of matter lies not in the particles' being alike, or in their working together, but in their coextensiveness.

Energy

The third significant thing about matter is energy. Energy is the mysterious something which holds the particles together and gives them the capacity for interaction. It is the most primitive form of stuff in the universe. However, energy must be further explained. There are two kinds of energy according to Teilhard. There is tangential energy, which can most easily be identified with what scientists usually call physical energy. Teilhard thought of this as the energy which is without, or external. There is also an internal, or within, energy which Teilhard calls radial energy. This might also be called a kind of spiritual or psychical energy. Radial energy is in every particle of matter scattered throughout the universe. He illustrates the two kinds of energy this way:

> 'To think, we must eat.' But what a variety of thoughts we get out of one slice of bread! Like the letters of the alphabet, which can equally well be assembled into nonsense as into

the most beautiful poem, the same calories seem as indifferent as they are necessary to the spiritual values they nourish.[2]

Teilhard is saying that physical energy is changed into thought. But this can only happen because there is also radial energy. Tangential energy relates to elements of the same complexity, while radial energy relates to making more complex the elements which are present.

The development of the structure of matter as described by the natural scientist is accepted by Teilhard at least as far as the natural scientist goes. Teilhard begins with his primordial particles (which to him were coextensive in the whole of the universe) and suggests that atoms are made out of these building blocks. These are the atoms which physicists describe. Also the primordial particles are probably not different from what physicists believe they have recently found track of—what they have called *quarks*. When a sufficient number of atoms are available in a stabilized form, they become the building blocks of the molecule. This unit of matter is the smallest which has a chemical identity. At the level of the molecules something new has appeared in the combination of the atomic particles, that is, minerals. When these molecules have multiplied until they become organic compounds, then they may be described as megamolecules. The megamolecule is not only much larger than the molecule but it is much more complex. Whereas molecules that have crystallized grow larger according to the same pattern, megamolecules differ according to a variety of patterns. Thereby they give birth to the novel and the new. These form the building blocks for the cells, the next step in the structure of matter within the structure of reality.

LAW

Laws are an integral part of the structure of reality. Teilhard does not make the distinction between statistical law and natural law which is most often done in the philosophy of science today. The reason for this is again the fact that Teilhard does not separate the descriptive and substantive sciences. He assumes, no doubt, that if there are various patterns which can be detected by the observation of statistics, there must be an ontological reason behind those statistics. Therefore he assumes an ontological basis for what he calls laws.

Law of the Conservation of Energy

The first important law for Teilhard is the common law of the conservation of energy. This law says that nothing is ever constructed unless there is an equivalent destruction.[3] This means that there is no change in the total amount of stuff in the universe. Though it may be organized differently from time to time or place to place, the total quantity of the matter and the energy of the universe does not vary. This is a commonly accepted law within the natural sciences. Only recently has it been challenged by astrophysicists who say that there may be a continual creation going on in the universe in order to supply the needed energy to keep the universe running.

Law of Entropy

For Teilhard the Second Law of Thermodynamics or the law of the dissipation of energy is also important. This law states that whenever there is a physical-chemical change, there is a loss of available usable energy in the form of heat, and the energy lost is irrecoverable. This does not mean that there is a destruction of anything, but rather that there is a change of form. This process is called entropy. The Second Law of Thermodynamics is one which Teilhard holds in common with the rest of the scientific community, but he has a novel way of utilizing it. He believes that entropy only operates upon tangential energy and not upon radial energy —that is, the law of the dissipation of energy only operates upon mechanical energy but not upon psychic energy.

This law plays an important part in Teilhard's whole scheme of the universe. It means that the universe is running out of available energy and that the time will come when it will no longer be a hospitable place for man, if man remains at his present place on the evolutionary scale. This makes it important for man to continue on to the next step toward which he is being driven by the purposive forces at work in the world.

Law of Complexity

The third law is what Teilhard calls the law of complexity. Science points out that there is a tendency for all things to become more and more complex with the passage of time. Every step higher on the scale of evolutionary appearances is accompanied by a higher degree of complexity. For example, an atom is a complex arrangement of whatever the primal stuff of the universe is. Molecules are made up of more or less complex arrangements of atoms, and cells are made up of somewhat complex arrangements of molecules. A fish is far more complex than a paramecium and a primate more complex than a fish.

There are two important points to be noted along with the law of complexity. One is that the degree of consciousness which is exhibited corresponds to the degree of complexity. Some have even called this the law of complexity-consciousness. Teilhard suggests that there is some degree of consciousness at every level of reality, even including the primordial stuff of the universe. He does not think that one should deny the existence of an atom just because human eyes are not sufficient instruments to see them, nor is it sufficient reason to deny consciousness in all things just because one is not able to examine and measure the degree of consciousness. As every bit of matter and energy turns in upon itself, it heightens the degree of consciousness. Thereby the highest degree of consciousness that we know is that which is in man, who is the most complex species.

The second point is that complexity brings to light thresholds where the new and the novel appear. When a piece of matter or energy turns in upon itself, becoming highly complex, it takes on new qualities. With complexification, we do not have merely a greater or a larger number of parts, but a new entity. It is here that the whole becomes greater than the sum of its parts. Where complexity develops to a given stage, a new level develops which utilizes the previous base. For instance, the particles become atoms; the atoms in a certain complexity become molecules. The molecules are put together in complexity and become megamolecules such as crystals. However, megamolecules not only add on indefinitely (as happens when you add megamolecules of crystals to megamolecules of crystals) but a new complexity can arise whereby comes life—megamolecules of protein combine to make a cell; and cells added to cells make an organism. By the same method you can go on to higher levels of reality. There is no doubt but that this law of complexity is the greatest essential to the whole scheme of Teilhard's thought.

CENTREISM

Centreism, the tendency of all things to converge, to move toward the center, is an important part of the structure of reality according to Teilhard. This means that ultimately there will be a totalization of all phenomena, whether physical, mental or spiritual. Totalization will be a kind of complete collectivism of all reality. This has not happened yet but it is in the process of happening, and the forces of centreism operate upon all phenomena, whatever their nature —material, energy or psychic. The eventual outcome of the process will be complete unity. This is not uniformity, but a unity in which everything becomes a part of a completed, organic whole, which is more than the sum of its parts— that is, something new. The word *implosion* describes this coming together of all things in centreism. Whereas an explosion pushes everything out toward the circumference, in implosion there is a sudden rush inward to the center. Although individual *explosions* may take place here or there, the ultimate direction and outcome of all things is *implosion*.

In his discussion of evolution Teilhard speaks about the apparent movement of all things outward in divergent patterns. One can see this if he looks at the growing diversity of living things from the first organic cells and organism.

Teilhard agrees that this emergence of new forms from a peduncle (the stem from which a new biological phylum emerges) does happen over and over again. But he also suggests that the structure of the universe causes these diverse movements from any peduncle to begin to converge after they reach their extremity. The ultimate destiny of any peduncle is convergence in a centric pattern. And convergence produces such an interwoven complex relationship that from this compression a threshold is crossed and the new and novel appears.

The structure of reality can also be described as dialectical. This is not a dialectical method of interpreting reality but rather for Teilhard the dialectic is a basic part of the structure of events and reality. Teilhard's dialectic is closely associated with his law of complexity, and occurs where there is movement from one level of reality to another. Whenever reality crosses a threshold and the novel and new appears, there is a demonstration of the dialectic at work. That is, opposing forms unite and create a new form. While there are many similarities between Teilhard and Marxism, there should be no confusion between the dialectic of Marx and Teilhard. Marx posited a dialectical materialism, whereas for Teilhard a basic "withinness" moves matter through whatever changes it undergoes. For him it is a dialectical spiritism or perhaps is more analogous to what William Temple called dialectical realism.

THE "WITHIN"

Several times already it has been necessary to speak of "withinness" when elaborating on some point in Teilhard's thought. For Teilhard, there is both the external nature of reality and also a withinness to or beneath that external reality, at every level. This withinness is the immeasurable part which Teilhard accuses the natural scientists of ignoring, even though it is evident from examining the evolutionary history of the microscopic period. Withinness is responsible for the principle of purpose (orthogenesis) which gives direction to all things and events. Withinness also might be identified with radial energy, inasmuch as radial energy is not measurable and is responsible for the inner drive of things. Perhaps it also can be identified with the mental or the spiritual which lies behind physical externalities. In Teilhard's thought, it is the force which unites all of the parts in the whole and brings about the coalescence of nature and history. It is impossible to overestimate the importance of withinness in the thought of Teilhard.

Purpose

Purpose is a part of the structure of reality. It might be argued from some of Teilhard's statements that purpose is that which is superimposed upon reality by God. From other statements one could also justify the view that God himself is a part of reality, even an important and dominating part, so that to say that God imposed purpose upon reality is not to imply that this was something artificial. Whether the withinness or energy that is a part of reality is identified with God or not, it is the nature of the psychic within matter to organize and direct nature and history purposefully.

Spirit

Teilhard's brief creed *What I Believe* elevates spirit. What has been said previously in this chapter about the structure of reality is just a refinement of the idea that ultimate reality is spirit. Spirit is the withinness that is behind all measurable things, and all measurable things are but the tangible expression of that spirit. Spirit is the quality that is behind all things, even the primordial stuff of the universe.

Personal

Reality must also be described as personal. There is a sense in which the personal is as ultimate as spirit, but more in a final sense than an original sense. All reality is being moved toward the personal, which has been the goal of all processes throughout the history of evolution. The personal arrived at its threshold with the appearance of man—which Teilhard calls *hominisation*. It continues to operate and be refined and will not cease until that which is fully personal—which might be called the superpersonal—arrives. It is the stage in which Christ will become All in All and therefore we will all be caught up in a personalized universe.

For Teilhard, reality cannot be looked upon as static. It is dynamic and characterized by dialectical thresholds and change. All of these changes have not taken place as yet, and the structure can only be sketched at this point.

III. Teilhard's Cosmology

Cosmology is important to Teilhard's thought. He sees the universe as the garden in which grows the prize fruit—the phenomenon of man. The principles which are active in the universe he sees as also active in the phenomenon of man.

CREATION

Perhaps the strangest thing about Teilhard's thought is the absence of any discussion about creation. There are many places where it would seem natural to discuss the original starting point of the universe, but Teilhard does not do so. It would take a hero-worshiper like Henri de Lubac to have enough imaginative piety to write a chapter on Teilhard entitled "Creation, Cosmogenesis, Christogenesis." [1] Piet Smulders also attempted a chapter entitled "Creation and Environment." [2] His chapter, however, gives an Old Testament theology of the doctrine of creation with barely a half dozen references to the works of Teilhard.

There is no doubt that Teilhard refers to God as creator, but what does he mean by that? In *Activation of Energy* he says:

> In a system of convergent cosmogenesis, to create is for God *to unite*. To unite, to form one with something, is to be

immersed in it; but to be immersed (in the plural) is to become a particle within it. And to become a particle in a world whose arrangement statistically entails disorder (and mechanically calls for effort) is to plunge into error and suffering, in order to overcome them.[3]

Teilhard goes on to discuss Christology, but the passage raises all sorts of prior questions. If to create is to unite, it seems that it is necessary to have something there first to unite. Therefore, is this really creation, at least in the sense in which Christian theology has spoken of *creatio ex nihilo* (creation out of nothing)? If, as Teilhard suggests, one of these prior things was God himself, Teilhard still has not dealt with the original starting point of matter. Does he purposely avoid *creatio ex nihilo?* Before going further, it must be said, in fairness to Teilhard, that very often he presents what he calls a "phenomenology"—a discussion of things as they are or appear to be—rather than trying to theologize or philosophize about a subject. It is true that he does not have the kind of empirical data about the original creation that he does about the mountain ranges, continents and oceans. However, even in his most phenomenological works (*The Phenomenon of Man*) he is able to show to his satisfaction nonempirical implications from empirical data.

Teilhard seems on the verge of discussing the creation of matter in *The Phenomenon of Man*. Under the subject "The Evolution of Matter" he has a subdivision entitled "The Appearance." However, it is evident in the following passage how far back he goes:

To begin with, at the very bottom there is still an unresolved simplicity, luminous in nature and not to be defined in terms of figures. Then, suddenly (?) came a swarming of elementary corpuscles, both positive and negative (protons, neutrons, electrons, photons): the list increases incessantly.[4]

From that point on he continues to discuss what he calls "the ascending evolution of atoms." [5]

Teilhard has much to offer both as the scientist and the religious thinker. Unfortunately on the doctrine of creation he is either silent or ambiguous. He speaks eloquently about the creation involved in the evolutionary process, but does not deal with the primeval origin of matter.

MATTER AND SPIRIT

Modern man has been caught in the debate between the reality of matter and the reality of spirit. Teilhard reflects on this problem in *The Activation of Energy:*

> Ever since man, in becoming man, started on his quest for unity, he has constantly oscillated, in his visions, in his ascesis, or in his dreams, between a cult of the spirit which made him jettison matter and a cult of matter which made him deny spirit. . . .[6]

Teilhard is not content to let the problem stop there because he accepts the reality of both matter and spirit. He sees a synthesis of the two as the ultimate goal of the universe, what he calls the Omega Point, and he calls the process *omegalization.* Therefore Teilhard can continue his evaluation of the history of the quarrel between matter and spirit by saying, ". . . omegalization allows us to pass between this Scylla and Charybdis of rarefaction or the quagmire." [7]

The matter-spirit issue is not an either/or issue with Teilhard. He sees spirit as a part of the withinness of matter. Spirit along with love is a kind of psychic energy without which all matter would collapse. Spirit also is an organizing force of matter.

Spirit should not be looked upon as a kind of extrinsic quality imposed upon matter and the world, because it is as much a part of matter and the world as skin is part of a hand. Scientists say that man is a product of the earth. Teilhard refuses to take away the spirit of man just because man is a product of the earth, for he sees spirit as much an integral part of the world as matter. Therefore, mind or intelligence is as much an integral part of man's coming out of the world as is man's body.

PANPSYCHISM

There are those who feel that for a priest Teilhard is too concerned with the world of matter and not enough with spirituality. Other observers, perhaps less sensitive to the necessity of theological language, evaluate Teilhard's thought as an immense mentalism rather than a materialism. In a footnote Hans Jonas says, "We may refer to the panpsychism of a Teilhard de Chardin, or (on a considerably higher philosophical plain) of Whitehead's theory of all actuality as 'feeling.'" [8] Jonas's theory is that in the history of thought there has been a movement from an early animism (that every object contains or is spirit) to a stage of dualism (where the world is divided into matter on the one hand and spirit on the other) to a monism which is either a materialism or an idealism (there is only one reality—either matter or some kind of spirit). Teilhard admits being a monist. However his monism is not a choice between materialism and idealism but a new synthesis or (as he speaks of it at times) a megasynthesis. It is the creation of a new sphere beyond the usual dualism or monism.

Teilhard often uses mystical phrases to express this truth. Here is an example from *Hymn of the Universe:*

> Rich with the sap of the world, I rise up towards the Spirit whose vesture is the magnificence of the material universe but who smiles at me from far beyond all victories; and, lost in the mystery of the flesh of God, I cannot tell which is the more radiant bliss: to have found the Word and so be able to achieve the mastery of matter, or to have mastered matter and so be able to attain and submit to the light of God. [9]

Teilhard tries to blur distinctions between matter and spirit. Again he puts it in poetic form: " 'Oh, the beauty of spirit as it rises up adorned with all the riches of the earth!' " [10]

Teilhard advocates orthogenesis, which is another term for his law of complexity. While Teilhard is in the minority believing in orthogenesis, he sees it as an absolute necessity in explaining the phenomenon of the universe and the phenomenon of man. Orthogenesis is the controlling activity by which there is an orderly maturing stage of a process. It is "the law of controlled complication," "the manifest property of living matter to form a system in which 'terms *succeed each other* experimentally, following constantly increasing degrees of *centro-complexity*'." [11] Teilhard believes that "orthogenesis is the dynamic and only complete form of heredity. Without orthogenesis life would only have spread; with it there is an ascent of life that is invincible." [12] He does not believe that nature is the blind fury which is depicted so often by artists, poets and even philosophers. While it is particularly pertinent to discuss orthogenesis as a biological concept in relation to the phenomenon of man, it cannot be overlooked in relation to the phenomenon of the universe, because the universe has not simply spread and moved at random but has been in a pattern of ascent.

As we have seen, Teilhard's description of the universe includes what he calls "the within," which is another way of describing the spiritual nature of matter.

When I speak of the *'within'* of the earth, I do not of course mean those material depths in which—only a few miles beneath our feet—lurks one of the most vexatious mysteries of science: the chemical nature and the exact physical condition of the internal regions of the globe. The *'within'* is used here . . . to denote the 'psychic' face of that portion of the stuff of the cosmos enclosed from the beginning of time within the narrow scope of the early earth. [13]

EVOLUTION OF THE COSMOS

The evolution of the cosmos is presented in three stages (spheres) by Teilhard—the geosphere, the biosphere, and the noosphere. The geosphere, the sphere of the earth, comes first in time. Millions of years ago a fragment broke loose from the sun but was not able to get outside the sun's gravitational field, and thus developed an elliptical orbit around the sun. That fragment, the earth, at first was still in the incandescent state of the stars. At those extremely high temperatures only the simplest states of matter can exist. We still see these states in the liquid metals of the *barysphere* at the center of the earth, and in the rarified gases of the stratosphere.

However, a cooling process went on, and eventually the outer edges of the fragment—at that time existing only as barysphere—began to cool. This allowed for the development of what Teilhard calls the *lithosphere* where the atoms could be transformed into inorganic molecules. The result was that a thin skin, the earth's crust, developed around the barysphere. This is the first envelope of the earth. Various gases escaped from the barysphere even through the thin crust of the lithosphere. Some of these gases were held on the surface of the lithosphere by the operation of gravity. Through a coalescence of these gases there developed the next sphere—the *hydrosphere*—surrounding the earth.

Some of the gases emitted from the barysphere escaped the most severe gravitational pull and formed yet another envelope around the earth. The most intense of the spheres beyond the hydrosphere was the *atmosphere* and the more rarified envelope was the *stratosphere*.

The evolution of the earth does not stop with the stratosphere, but goes on to the *biosphere* and the *noosphere*. These are the spheres of life in all its forms, and of mind or thought. They were built upon the structure of the physical earth and depend upon it. For Teilhard, the forming of the earth is shot through with purposiveness—the earth evolved so that the biosphere and the noosphere could rise.

While it leaves the chapter on Teilhard's cosmology incomplete, discussions of the biosphere, noosphere and the personalized universe will be discussed later in order to put them in their proper perspectives. Then the reader can complete this exercise in Teilhard's cosmology.

IV. Teilhard's God

Leaving out of consideration Teilhard's letters, there is surprisingly little direct mention of God in Teilhard's writings. This is at least partly the result of his works being an apologetic task rather than a theological exercise. While Teilhard underlines the fact that his world and system do not hold together without an understanding of and belief in God, his works are not meant to build a confessional understanding of the doctrine of God.

Then, too, Teilhard's works are largely anthropologically centered. This is also the result of his apologetic task. He is not attempting to be a secular humanist, although there might be justification in calling him a Christian humanist. Nor is he trying to bring God in by the back door. Rather, when one has seen the pattern of Teilhard's understanding of man and the universe, the intuition comes clearly that there is "something" that holds the whole picture together that is beyond both man and the universe.

When Teilhard does bring the focus upon God, there is little to remind one of traditional dogmatics. (This is still making an exception of the personal, nontechnical letters which Teilhard wrote to friends and relatives.) This might be because he felt that many of the dogmatic categories had become so rigid and thoroughly defined that it would be difficult for their precise definitions to fit into the new approach which his system represents, and the new language he used. Teilhard was loyal to the church and to tradition, and while not denying the richness of the past, he was trying to infuse new life and philosophical breath into the church. What he created was not a philosophical-theological system in the historic sense of those terms, but an entirely new system (as new as any system can be)—the Teilhardian synthesis.

Traditional theologies begin with the doctrine of God and his revelation, and on the basis of those explain the world and man. Teilhard begins with the artifacts of the world, develops an anthropology, and then a cosmic picture. This is not an attempt to prove God in the scholastic tradition by starting with the world and ending with a proven existence of God. Teilhard starts with the empirical data and shows how there is a mystery within this data which holds it all together. Several interpreters have compared Teilhard to St. Augustine, and with good reason. Teilhard does not deny his faith in God by starting with the empirical and anthropological, just as Augustine realized that his understanding of God began with himself—his confrontation with God which led to confession and prayer.

THE PHILOSOPHICAL-THEOLOGICAL TRADITION

Teilhard's view of God is akin to idealism, although there is also disparity between the two. The idealist view of God tends to make him the principle at work in every function and at every level of the universe. The philosophical idealist may think of God as the amorphous power which permeates every particle and event of the universe. This view tends to be that of romantic idealists such as Coleridge. Teilhard also sees God as being a substratum of reality and the One who formed the events of the world, but he would take exception to the idealist's amorphism. While Teilhard says "Christ, principle of universal vitality," [1] he is thinking of

God as the center of convergence who guides, directs, and permeates every event rather than being the sum total of diffusion.

Teilhard's God can be compared to the God of the existentialists for two reasons. First, Teilhard's emphasis is upon act, action and energy rather than on a kind of platonic, static, removed being or substance. Second, Teilhard's God is like Tillich's Ground of Being upon which all things are dependent. For both Teilhard and the existentialists, nothing is profane in and of itself, because there is the element of the sacred beneath. Teilhard, however, probably outdoes the existentialists, because his idea is that everything is really sacred regardless of whether man calls it profane or not. It does not depend upon man's relationship to Being or the Ground of Being to make something sacred or profane, but according to Teilhard there is Divine presence in every thing and every act. For Teilhard, the existentialists' God is usually too much an impersonal Ground of Being or an impersonal Being or the impersonal great act of becoming. Rather than depersonalize God, Teilhard wishes to personalize the whole universe, and the pattern for that is a superpersonal God.

If there is a philosophical and theological school in which Teilhard should be placed, it is probably that of process theology and philosophy, which defines reality dynamically and as an ever growing phenomenon. The influence in this direction was not so much Whitehead or Bergson, though if one understands the inner dynamic in the writings of Bergson, he will be a long way toward understanding the extreme of consciousness and radial energy in Teilhard. The "creative force" (*élan vital*) of Bergson comes the closest of any non-Teilhardian language to describing the God of Teilhard. Teilhard used other terms to describe the *élan vital* rather than the specific term *God*. Process theology, however, is descriptive of Teilhard's God in a way that Bergson's philosophy is not. That is because process theology sees God caught up in the process of the creation of ultimate reality. This is

comparable to Teilhard's idea that there will be the convergence of all realities at the Omega Point. Teilhard suggests that the future is as real as the past, so that God is not
a lesser being gaining strength and momentum but he is the
power and the vital force throughout the whole process.

Even in terms of theology, Teilhard qualifies his view of
God. He says about the Christian that "whether he lives or
dies, *by* his life and *by* his death, he in some sense completes
his God, and is at the same time mastered by him." [2]

PSEUDONYMS FOR GOD

The heading I have used here, "Pseudonyms for God," carries with it some ambiguity. That ambiguity is purposeful
because it is not always easy to decide whether certain words
Teilhard uses are really expressions by which he means
"God." Also, he may seem to refer to God at one time, but
at others may mean something entirely different from God.
Some of his words have an evolutionary character, where at
one point in the historical spectrum they mean less than God
but at another point they mean God.

Love

The word *love* is one of the words which from time to
time appears to be a pseudonym for God. As a pseudonym
for God it might be written off because it could be interpreted that Love is one of the characteristics of God. However, Teilhard devotes a section of his book, *The Phenomenon
of Man*, to the subject, "Love as Energy." [3] Love as energy is
the "withinness of things" and is closely comparable to
Bergson's *élan vital*. Love is the energy that totalizes, social-
izes, and ultrapersonalizes. This is the energy which moves
within things (radial energy) driving them toward the goal
of convergence and ultimately the Omega Point. What else
can love be but that energy and power which is the Divine

presence and providence giving purpose and guidance to all
things?

Strangely enough, it is in the section of Teilhard's writings
called "Love, The Historical Product of Human Evolution" [4]
that Teilhard says:

> Many times already (and especially at the dawn of the
> Christian era) the religious gropings of humanity had drawn
> near to this idea that God, a spirit, could only be reached by
> spirit. But it is in Christianity alone that the movement
> achieves its definitive expression and content. The gift of
> the heart in place of the prostration of the body; communion
> beyond sacrifice; God is love, and only to be finally reached
> in love; this is the psychological revolution, and the secret
> of the triumph of Christianity.[5]

Teilhard probably would never have been embarrassed by the
use of *Love* and *God* as synonymous. Christopher Mooney in
Teilhard de Chardin and the Mystery of Christ sees that God
as Love is more than a characteristic of God, just as spirit
is more than a characteristic of God.

Spirit

Spirit is another word which Teilhard often uses for
"withinness" and the psychic energy. He does not mean by it
a quality either of man or of the earth, but rather that spirit
is the essence, the heart of, the very center of and the reality
of all else.

> . . . spirit is neither superimposed nor accessory to the
> cosmos, but that it quite simply represents the higher state
> assumed in and around us by the primal and indefinable
> things that we call, for want of a better name, the 'stuff of
> the universe.' Nothing more; and also nothing less. Spirit is
> neither a meta- nor an epi-phenomenon; it is *the* phenome-
> non.[6]

It is this spirit which gives life to everything.

> . . . scientifically speaking, there are no *spirits* in nature.
> But there is *a spirit*, physically defined by a certain tension of

consciousness on the surface of the earth. This animated
covering of our planet may with advantage be called the
biosphere—or more precisely (if we are only considering
its thinking fringe) the noosphere.[7]

This spirit is the interior force which has given the dynamic
and guidance for all that has happened in moving things
toward the future convergent state. Ultimately there will be
a transformation of all into a state of spirituality.

It is difficult to prove that Teilhard really means to identify
spirit with God. It is too much like a neo-Platonic emanation
by which he is trying to have the advantage of the Divine
as a part of withinness without God's direct involvement
and responsibility for all that happens in the world.

Teilhard speaks of God's spiritual function in terms of the
reality of movement. He understands this mobility in the
following way:

> The first condition is that He shall combine in his singu-
> larity the evolutionary extension of all the fibres of the world
> in movement: a God of cosmic synthesis in whom we can be
> conscious of advancing and joining together by spiritual
> transformation of all the powers of matter.[8]

Therefore, God's spirituality is the movement of all things
toward the convergence which is the state of spiritual transformation. Thereby one defines spirituality as the Divine
presence in the world in the past and the present which is
being attracted by the spirituality of the future.

Christosphere

It is frustrating for a dogmatic theologian to examine the
technical works of Teilhard and try to determine how his
Christology develops systematically. The reader of Teilhard,
however, will immediately be struck by the fact that his preoccupation is with Christ and not Jesus or Jesus Christ. Even
the passages which speak of the Incarnation have a strange

non-Galilean ring to them. Teilhard says that "for ninety percent of those who view Him from outside, the Christian God looks like a great landowner administering his estates, the world." He goes on, however, to give another evaluation: "The essence of Christianity is neither more nor less than a belief in the implication of the world in God by the incarnation." [9] Incarnation for Teilhard means that God has come into the world and is God with us. He has clothed himself in the universe so that it is all now the body of Christ. The Incarnation of God has transformed the whole world into a sacred world.

As the body and blood are transformed during the Holy Eucharist into the actual body and blood of Jesus Christ, according to the Roman Catholic doctrine of transubstantiation, so Teilhard believes that in the Incarnation, by his own passions and sufferings, Christ offered up the whole world as a sacrifice to God. What happens to the individual elements according to transubstantiation happened to the entire universe in the Incarnation.

It is interesting that Christopher Mooney in his book, *Teilhard de Chardin and the Mystery of Christ,* has a section which he calls "Jesus of Nazareth as a Personal Centre." [10] This is more Christopher Mooney's eisegesis than the technical thought of Teilhard. There is only one pertinent footnote in the section by Mooney and it refers to a personal letter of Teilhard rather than to one of his technical works.

It is not Jesus of Nazareth who occupies the center of Teilhard's attention but the cosmic Christ. One can see a parallel in Teilhard's thinking between the spirit and the cosmic Christ. Teilhard writes not only about the presence of the cosmic Christ that energizes, gives purpose and direction to all things, but he also refers to a Christogenesis and Christosphere. Just as in the past, various particles converged and at a critical point crossed a critical threshold into a new sphere which was not an available precise entity previously—as for instance convergence of particles of gases

brought about the hydrosphere—so convergence is still at
work at the present time. And eventually convergence will
develop into a Christosphere. This will be the climax which
will be the Omega Point where God will be all in all.

Omega Point

The last of the pseudonyms for God is the Omega Point,
from the biblical symbolism of alpha and omega, the first and
last letters of the Greek alphabet (see Rev: 1:8; 21:6). The
Omega Point resembles the goal of Aristotelian teleology
where everything moves toward a final state. The Omega
Point is the sign of climax of the forces of convergence,
which brings all spirit, matter, energy, love into the final
supertotalization and superpersonalization which will be God.

While Teilhard talks about God in the present tense, he
discusses the Omega Point as a future convergence. He does
not mean that the Omega Point will swallow up all that went
before, because he considers it a critical threshold in which
everything will become synthesized. Neither is he a process
theologian who sees God as a limited entity struggling to hold
things together. What does he mean to say? Teilhard never
clarifies his discussion. Perhaps the greatest disservice which
Teilhard's superiors did to him was not that they stopped the
publication of his works during his lifetime (after all, they
have been published since his death and are very popular),
but that they did not allow him public exposure so that his
statements and views could be debated in the public forums
of the press, universities and seminaries where he could have
explained, clarified or sharpened any of his points.

GOD AS PERSONAL

Christian theology has always maintained, as a distinctive
belief, the existence of a personal God. Christian theologians
who have written or spoken contrary to that idea have often
found themselves in difficulties both with their peers and

their confessional groups. Creeds as well as dogmatics have emphasized the personal nature of God. The fact that the Incarnation is central to Christianity has made this an indelible part of its faith and practice. Of course Teilhard was aware of this. He was very sensitive about this point because he was subject to misunderstanding. Christian mystics and scientists often have difficulty with the doctrine of the person of Jesus Christ. Not only was Teilhard both a mystic and a scientist, but his system also is one which attempts to identify an inner energy and a future convergence with the Divine. Therefore Teilhard emphasizes the many ways that he seeks to speak of God as personal.

Teilhard recognizes that "the personality of God (together with the survival of the 'soul') calls out the greatest opposition and antipathy from contemporary scientific thought." He is willing to stand against these scientific prejudices and opposition, and points out to the scientists that by the main event of hominisation (the species reaching the point of man), the most advanced portion of the cosmos has become personalized. He does not stop here but goes on to say that

> since everything *in the universe beyond man* takes place within *personalized being,* the final divine term of universal convergence must also (eminently) possess the quality of a person (without which it would be inferior to the elements it governs).[11]

Recognizing that there is a problem when he talks about the crossing of the threshold at the Omega Point where God will be all in all, he faces it in this way:

> The final summit of the perfected—that is to say personalized—world (that is to say God) can in no way be conceived as born of a sort of aggregation of elementary personalities (since these are, by nature, irremovable from their own centres). In order to super-animate without destroying a universe formed of personal elements, it must be a special centre itself.[12]

Rather than suggesting that God is impersonal or that his personality is destroyed in the aggregation at the final convergence, Teilhard speaks of the continued personality or perhaps superpersonality of God. He puts it very emphatically in *The Phenomenon of Man:* "In the centre, so glaring as to be disconcerting, is the uncompromising affirmation of a personal God. . . ." [13] As a matter of fact Teilhard entitles one whole chapter, "Beyond the Collective: The Hyper-Personal." [14]

PANTHEISM

One of the most repeated criticisms of Teilhard has been that he was a pantheist. The accusation arises out of his view that God through the spirit, radial energy, is present in the world and within all matter, guiding the world toward its end or goal. That goal has also been criticized as pantheistic, because Teilhard describes it as a Christosphere, the Omega Point, where God is all in all. In the last paragraph of the text of his magnum opus, *The Phenomenon of Man*, Teilhard deals with the subject of pantheism forthrightly.

> Lastly, to put an end once and for all to the fears of 'pantheism,' constantly raised by certain upholders of traditional spirituality as regards evolution, how can we fail to see that, in the case of a *converging universe*, such as I have delineated, far from being born from the fusion and confusion of the elemental centres it assembles, the universal centre of unification (precisely to fulfil its motive, collective and stabilising function) must be conceived as pre-existing and transcendent. A very real 'pantheism' if you like (in the etymological meaning of the word) but an absolutely legitimate pantheism—for if, in the last resort, the reflective centres of the world are effectively no more than 'one with God,' this state is obtained not by identification (God becoming all) but by the differentiating and communicating action of love (God all *in everyone*). And that is essentially orthodox and Christian. [15]

The problem of a personal God is closely related to the problem of pantheism. If Teilhard fails to build the case for a personal God, then he falls victim to pantheism. If his analysis of the kind of superpersonalization of God which in turn transforms the world into a superpersonalized state is correct, then he not only makes God personal with a center (concentrated, not diffused), but also provides for centers other than God, even though God is "all in all." This is what he means when he says,

> By its structure Omega, in its ultimate principle, can only be a *distinct Centre radiating at the core of a system of centres;* a grouping in which personalisation of the All and personalisations of the elements reach their maximum, simultaneously and without merging, under the influence of a supremely autonomous focus of union.[16]

Teilhard warns us not to confuse individuality with personality, because often the confusion results in an egoism which may be racial or nonracial. Personality is different and other than individuality.

A further question should be raised—whether or not the ultimate outcome is apotheosis (all becoming divinized) rather than pantheism. One of the reasons for raising this question is the passage in *Building the Earth:*

> Is there not now under way one further metamorphosis, the ultimate one, the realization of God at the heart of the Noosphere, the passage of the circles to their common Centre: the apparition of the 'Theosphere'? [17]

The question may very well be "Is the Omega Point not the final step in the divinizing process which has gone on all through history; the point toward which the spirit has been driving the universe?" For Teilhard, the world is not God but is being transformed into the sacred.

One of the more sublime passages in *The Phenomenon of Man* sums up the problem of pantheism:

Christ, principle of universal vitality because sprung up as man among men, put himself in the position (maintained ever since) to subdue under himself, to purify, to direct and superanimate the general ascent of consciousness into which he inserted himself. By a perennial act of communion and sublimation, he aggregates to himself the total psychism of the earth. And when he has gathered everything together and transformed everything, he will close in upon himself and his conquests, thereby rejoining, in a final gesture, the divine focus he has never left. Then as St. Paul tells us, *God shall be all in all.* This is indeed a superior form of 'pantheism' without trace of the poison of adulteration or annihilation: the expectation of perfect unity, steeped in which each element will reach its consummation at the same time as the universe.[18]

The God of Teilhard is no simple person or being. The complexities will become even more apparent in the chapters that follow.

V. Teilhard's Anthropology

As a trained geologist, Pierre Teilhard de Chardin studied and was well versed in palaeontology, the science of early forms of life in other geologic periods as recorded in fossil remains. He published more in this area than in geology proper. It is ironic, however, that his current fame is related to the area of biology, even though this was not his specialty. Of course, this biology has philosophical and theological ramifications.

THE EVOLUTIONARY BACKGROUND OF MAN

Evolution is a central theme of Teilhard's work. He takes for granted that evolution is fact, not fanciful imagination or hypothesis or, at its best, a theory. His whole program stands or falls on the reality of evolution.

Teilhard sums up the current question by saying that all scientists tend now to believe in some sort of evolution. "Whether or not that evolution is *directed* is another question. Asked whether life is *going anywhere* at the end of its transformations, nine biologists out of ten will today say no, even passionately." [1]

Teilhard is just as adamant that the process of evolution has been directed purposefully. He accuses Darwin and his followers of a kind of fixity which cannot account for the phenomenon of man and the constant movement (over the long period of time) from the simple to the complex, the brutish to the intellectual, the isolated to the social.

Orthogenesis is of course at the root of Teilhard's program. It is through orthogenesis that there is purpose and movement forward. This is the result of transformism. Teilhard usually explains it in terms of spirit, or love, or Christ.

Scientists debate Teilhard's orthogenesis, just as vigorously as theologians debate his Christology and eschatology. P. G. Fothergill, sometime senior lecturer in botany at the University of Newcastle, examines the question in a stimulating and learned article.[2] Some biologists have reacted violently against the theory of orthogenesis. Several others are sympathetic with it although perhaps in a cautious and redefined way. While Fothergill acknowledges that there are those who do not take Teilhard's orthogenesis literally or seriously, he demonstrates from some of Teilhard's major works and last papers that Teilhard sees it as important if not necessary for his whole system.

THE PHENOMENON OF PLANET EARTH

In chapter III we discussed the evolution of the cosmos and particularly of the earth, from an incandescent piece of the sun through the various stages or spheres, from barysphere, through lithosphere and hydrosphere to atmosphere and stratosphere.

For the development of man, it is the hydrosphere that is important. The hydrosphere produced the place and the correct temperatures and chemical conditions for the next step of development. Little grains of protein began to form and eventually cover densely the surface of the earth in the water. At this point the law of complexity asserted itself, organizing the grains of protein into increasingly complex forms in a convergent pattern, so that eventually they crossed a critical threshold to become a new level or sphere, the level of organic cells—life. The threshold was reached for all the cells at one given moment, because the conditions would not be exactly right for the change at more than one time. Teilhard believes that this new state arrived in order to give better survival amidst the crushing competition within the previous form.

The new level Teilhard terms the *biosphere*. With life came the further developments of viruses, blood tissue and connective tissue. There are three branches of life: vegetable, insect and vertebrate. It is the vertebrate branch to which attention must be given, because out of it men came. The first development was the world of fish. After some time there began to appear dry land with the eruption of volcanoes and the movement of the thin crust of the earth. The fish with limb-like fins and some lung fish which had the capacity to live out of their usual environment became the amphibians of the Permian Period.

An interiorization began under the law of complexity-consciousness. There was the development of the spinal cord and the central nervous system. This could not happen among the insects because they are too small to have enough of a central nervous system to become the physiological basis of man. Neither did it happen among such animals as dinosaurs because, although they were huge, their brains were little more than nodules on a spinal cord. Finally the intensity of the complexification reached a new state of consciousness which Teilhard calls the *noosphere*. It is here that man appears as man. The noosphere marks the hominisation of man.[3]

THE PHENOMENON OF MAN

At the heart of his discussion of the phenomenon of man is Teilhard's presupposition about the reality of transformism. He says at one point that on the general and fundamental fact that organic evolution exists, applicable equally to life as a whole or to any given living creature in particular, all scientists are today in agreement for the very good reason that they couldn't practice science if they thought otherwise.[4]

In the matter of evolution Teilhard speaks to two of the most used criticisms of evolution. One is that there are missing links which the evolutionists have not been able to produce. Teilhard dismisses this because beginnings are always fragile and weak, and structure is precarious. The first forms are easily destroyed by time. This happens in the world of invented mechanisms also. Where are the first buggies or covered wagons or even automobiles? Often a whole generation of invented objects are lost before any are preserved. In biology a peduncle—the beginning stem of a form of life— is obscured by the phylum which it produces. Once the phylum is assured, it is not possible to distinguish the characteristics which were present in the peduncle prior to the phylum.[5]

The second argument that is used against evolution is that we do not see any new species evolving now. For Teilhard, this is not an argument against his view of evolution but rather one for it. During the earliest stages, the evolutionary process was constantly in a state of divergence where many false branches were being put out. Only in the relatively recent history of the world has this divergence slowed down and only stopped over the very short range. Instead of divergence, the universe is now in a period in which all things are converging. It is out of convergence, centreity and complexity that Teilhard believes will come the next sphere.

Teilhard's view of transformism is not that of old Darwinianism or the present Neo-Darwinianism (commonly known as the modern synthetic theory), but is based for the most part on a Neo-Lamarckianism. However Lamarckianism has been rejected by most twentieth-century scientists with the notable exceptions of Lysenko and Lecomte du Nouy.[6]

To trace the history of the anthropoids, culminating in man, Teilhard uses his background in palaeontology, geology, and anthropology. Man appeared at the end of the Tertiary age, approximately one million years ago. At this critical threshold, as for the previous ones, the conditions necessary for the development of man as we know him were only available for a short time. This leads Teilhard to believe that the species man appeared at one moment. This is true whether there was just one set of human pairings (monogenism) or whether there were similar developments which happened in China, Europe, Africa and Australia.

Teilhard notes some important factors in hominisation. The consciousness and psychic capacity which is in all matter became more concentrated with the increasing complexity of the earth spheres and of living creatures. The idea of centreity is essential here. The consciousness at minute levels of matter is increased as matter centers in on itself, and as a result, there is much greater consciousness apparent in mammals. And at the stage when one can say for sure that man has arrived, there one finds the appearance of *reflective* thought. The difference is that an animal knows but man knows that he knows.

One of the prerequisites for the birth of reflective thought was the development of a place where thought could become intense, the cranium. In early types of pre-man (such as australopithecus), the cranial capacity was rather small. This was because the heavy jaws required thick maxillary muscles in the top part of the head. By the time of Neanderthal Man the jaws were much more vertically free, allowing for a much larger cranial capacity and leaving room for the development of what is known as the frontal lobe. By the time of Cromagnon Man we have true man with a full cranial capacity.

The increased cranial capacity allowed for intensity of

thought, centreity and ramification to take place. Through the history of pre-man there was very little change in the part of his brain which had to do with motor activity. Cranial growth was in the area which produces reflective thought. The law of complexity-consciousness comes into play here. As the brain becomes more complex, a new step in the history of the world is taken, and a new species—man—appears which is capable of reflective thought. This did not just come by the exterior addition of matter upon matter but by the withinness of reality. Teilhard says, "By the end of the Tertiary era, the psychical temperature in the cellular world has been rising for more than 500 million years." It was time for man to appear and only a "tiny 'tangential' increase" was needed so that the " 'radial' was turned back on itself and so to speak took an infinite leap forward. Outwardly, almost nothing in the organs changed. But in depth, a great revolution had taken place: consciousness was now leaping and boiling in a space of super-sensory relationships and perceptions; and simultaneously consciousness was capable of perceiving itself. . . ." [7] A new species had arrived.

With the new species began the *noosphere*. As there was an envelope of water, the hydrosphere, around the world, out of which developed the atmosphere and the stratosphere, so there has developed an envelope of thought. Now there are minute grains of thought scattered all over the surface of the earth, producing *noogenesis*, which is the birth and development of this sphere of thought in the world. The newest sphere continues to intensify and become complete.

Orthogenesis is a concept basic to this system. Orthogenesis says that change is not completely random but that there is purpose working in every change of species and phyla. The processes of changes are directed. There is within matter itself a withinness (radial energy) which exerts a sense of direction. Therefore all things tend to become more complex, organized and given to consciousness. For Teilhard, orthogenesis must be given this wide scope of interpretation.

The geneticists and biochemists who oppose the idea of orthogenesis are concerned with the minute specific explanations
of the minute evolutionary processes which they see in their
laboratory. At this level there is no need for an orthogenetic
presupposition. This would only be likely to come from
someone such as Teilhard who was a palaeontologist and
who saw the direction of the movement of change and was not
concerned with the specific mechanism of change.[8]

Evolution is still going on. Teilhard does not mean by the
word *man* only an abstraction or generalization of a species
in which there are many individuals. He also means that
there was a development which was *Man* (with a capital
"M") or if you wish, Mankind, meaning a special being
instead of a class name for many individuals. Within the
phylum "man" there was divergence as a result of tangential
energy, developing various races and nationalities. However,
reflective thought, as a result of the "within" or radial energy,
is bringing about convergence. Since every particle of matter
is coextensive with every other particle of matter and the
universe, thought cannot be isolated. Therefore the envelope
of thought around the world is a reality, and it brings with
it a companion reality, *Man*. You have many particles of
matter which go together to make up an atom; many atoms
which go together to make up a molecule; many molecules
which go together to make up a megamolecule; and many
megamolecules which make up living beings. In the same
way you have many seeds of thought or grains of thought
which make up still another larger reality, the noosphere. So
all of the individual men are also the atomistic realities which
make up the larger reality of *Man*.

VI. The Implications of Teilhard's Thought for Social Philosophy

It is necessary to discuss the implications of Teilhard's thought for social philosophy because of the crushing weight of social problems in the twentieth century. The problems of atomic energy, urbanization, communication, genetics, population, and war force any religionist who wishes to have a word from God in our day to deal with the destiny of Man as well as the destiny of men.

This chapter will be limited to the examination of the implications of Teilhard's thought for several important social structures which are present in contemporary human society. "Social structure" will not necessarily connote a static system. Teilhard's system is very dynamic in contrast to the static world-view of medieval science and theology or the semi-static world-view of Darwinian "fixity" evolution. "Social structures" in this chapter mean the framework (either as it is or as some would have it be) of the relationships between men and between their institutions. Unfortunately the length of this chapter does not allow relating Teilhard's thought to two areas of current social sensitivity: race and marriage (especially the role of women).

SOCIALIZATION AND COLLECTIVISM

Socialization is an important concept in Teilhard's thought. The principle of socialization is at work in the lowest forms of matter, and the socialization of man is the apex of evolution. All bits of matter tend to aggregate and form "societies" of atoms, molecules and cells. Socialization is either the end result or the final form of interiorization, reflection, complexification, convergence, collectivization and totalization. Although socialization is evident at lower levels of reality, it is heightened at the level of hominisation. Teilhard says that " 'human socialisation . . . is the very axis of the cosmic vortex of interiorisation which is pursuing its course.' " [1]

Several reasons might be given for the origin of society: the need to cooperate for protection, for artificial structures, for population expansion and aggression. If society is the result of any one of these reasons, when the need passes, society can cease. If society is the result of aggression or is artificial, then, as Rousseau suggested, it is the duty of man to do away with society. Teilhard suggests that rather than these artificial explanations, society is natural, the result of the socialization principle which causes all things to aggregate and converge. It would be not only undesirable but impossible to do away with society, since socialization is ingrained within the nature of all reality and most evidently within man.

Teilhard's idea of socialization means that society should become more and more complex. He would never demand with Rousseau a "return to nature" nor a romantic "back to the simple life." He would not care to eliminate the "red tape" bureaucracy but would only want to make it more efficient and extend it to all parts of society, inasmuch as it is the outcome of complexification and socialization. Teilhard thinks that structures and institutions are signs of man's maturity and not his decadence (as so many are inclined to say today). These structures are indications of the intensity present in recent stages of socialization and demonstrate an advanced degree of hominisation.

The principles of centreity and socialization inevitably led Teilhard to a collectivism which he saw as part of every level of reality. The tendency of convergence in matter leads to a collectivism which in man produces consciousness—mind.[2] Teilhard states it this way:

> In the passage of time, a state of collective human consciousness has been progressively evolved which is inherited by each succeeding generation of conscious individuals, and to which each generation adds something.[3]

Although the principle of collectivism is applicable at all levels of reality, according to Teilhard it is most fully operative at the human level in socialization.

> Collectivisation . . . takes the form of the all-encompassing ascent of the masses; the constant tightening of economic bonds; the spread of financial and intellectual association; the totalisation of political regimes; the closer physical contact of individuals as well as of nations; the increasing impossibility of being or acting or thinking *alone*—in short, the rise, in every form, of the *Other* around us. We are all constantly aware of these tentacles of a social condition that is rapidly evolving to the point of becoming monstrous.[4]

Collectivism raises the specter of Marxism and communism because it is one of the central themes of communism. Some theologians have become alarmed because collectivism is so important in Teilhard's thought. A word such as *comradeship* sounds Marxist. But Teilhard uses other phrases along with it, such as, "we are to avoid the road of brute material force" and "friendly rivalry." [5] These help differentiate Teilhard from Marxism. He points out some of the basic differences between his thought and Marxism when he writes:

> *In the marxist quarter,* I would not hesitate to say that it is very clearly the spirit of centration which is striving to emerge through the 'communist' effort, in order to super-differentiate man and super-organize the earth. 'Striving to emerge,' I say advisedly; but it will never succeed in doing

so until the party theoreticians make up their minds at last to accord to the superstructure of the world the final consistence which they still confine to the material infra-structure of things.[6]

If collectivism in Teilhard is linguistically different from collectivism in Marxism, is there a philosophical difference? A major difference between Teilhard and Marxism is that for Teilhard the material is the basic internal structure, not the ultimate superstructure which for him is Spirit, Christosphere, or Omega Point.[7] For the Marxist the basic *and* the ultimate is matter. Therefore, for Teilhard, the ultimate of collectivism is something qualitatively different than matter; it is not a superorganization of society. The ultimate collectivism is complete socialization that crosses the threshold into another organic reality which is a spiritual reality. That new reality is the Christosphere or Omega Point which transcends Marxists' matter and their superorganization of society.

The close affinity between a Christian writer and Marxism should not surprise anyone. Many theologians, notably Paul Tillich, have pointed out the affinity between Christianity and Marxism, showing that Marxism has secularized Christian symbols.[8]

UTOPIANISM

The dream of a utopian society has appeared often since Plato wrote his *Republic,* and Plato was preceded by the utopian dreams of Old Testament men. Josiah, Isaiah, Jeremiah, Ezekiel and Ezra all envisioned a perfected society. Although the original tribal division of Palestine was probably the result of *Realpolitik,* it was later idealized as a kind of utopian society.

Closer to our time, the nineteenth century's belief in the inevitability of progress proved fertile soil for utopian dreamers, but their dreams were shattered by the First World

War. The rise of technology produced not only dreams of utopia but warnings about such technological societies. Huxley's *Brave New World* and George Orwell's *1984* are two of the best known. Influenced by political realism and positivism, philosophers now reject utopian speculation, as do theologians, influenced by Barthianism. In his book *The Uncommitted,* however, Kenneth Keniston denies that Americans have lost their utopian thinking; it has been transvalued, he says, into private utopias (the "privatization of utopia") such as recreation, leisure time, art, poetry and hobbies.[9] On the other hand, Teilhard admits to being utopian, because

> it is finally the utopians, not the 'realists,' who make scientific sense. They at least, though their flights of fancy may cause us to smile, have a feeling for the true dimensions of the phenomenon of man.[10]

Teilhard's belief in utopianism is different from a great deal of utopian thought which has tended to come from an individual, local attempt to create an ideal society by isolating the community from the rest of the world. A recent example of such utopian isolation can be seen in counter-culture youth who drop out from "society" and form communes—their own type of utopia. Theodore Roszak points out that these young people have been misunderstood. "How often," he asks, "have we heard old-line radicals condemn the bohemian young for the 'irresponsibility' of their withdrawal into kooky communities of their own?"[11] Whereas, former utopians tried to transform the world, these youth (commonly called "hippies") just try to "make do" (in the phraseology of the utopian, Paul Goodman[12]) with the little bit of the world available to them. Martin Buber describes these youthful utopians when he evaluates current utopian attitudes as "resistance to mass or collective loneliness."[13] All such retreats from society are contrary to Teilhard's principles of convergence and socialization, and he would call them contrary to the nature of all reality.

The two current major utopian systems are communism and Christian millenarianism. Teilhard's utopian theory belongs to neither group but arises from his belief that there is purpose within the basic structure of reality. Observing the changes from the early beginnings of life to the present stage of hominisation, one has to admit that there has been progress, including the birth and growth of morality through the principles of love, convergence, complexification and consciousness. Seeing that it takes purpose to explain the progress evident thus far, Teilhard supposes that this purpose will continue to drive history until utopia is realized.

DEMOCRACY AND TOTALITARIANISM

Teilhard's sympathies were naturally on the side of the democracies inasmuch as he was a Frenchman. However, he was also a member of a totalitarian confessional group—the Society of Jesus—so that his life-situation gave him the emotional freedom to criticize the democratic structures.

Teilhard saw limitations in a democratic structure. While he recognized the value of individual human rights, he noted the necessity of common human enterprises and even hinted that democracies were based upon anarchy rather than human cooperation.[14] If this is the case, modern democracies are a step backward.

Democracies take pluralism for granted, while Teilhard opposes pluralism as a solution to the human problem. Such pluralism isolates people from one another when there needs to be the interaction of people in complete socialization. He feels that this is only a temporary step towards the totalization of humanity.[15]

Another problem with the democracies, according to Teilhard, is that they have an incomplete, ambiguous, ill-defined and static concept of justice to which they are dedicated. Teilhard believes that the destiny of man must be more powerful than this ambiguity. If the concepts are static, they will be by-passed and will soon be out of date. What Teilhard proposes is a more dynamic sense of human destiny (although it might be argued whether his is any less ambiguous or better defined).

One of democracy's strong points is the place it gives to the individual. However, Teilhard holds that individualism has become the subtle replacement for personalism. Because of this, "democracy, rather than freeing man, has merely emancipated him." [16] Something more positive is needed than isolating men from one another. According to Teilhard, the individual units (man) must make up a whole organism (society).

Teilhard sees some positive elements in the democracies. He points out the internationalism of communism and the democracies as being superior to the particularism of the Axis powers (although the Axis powers later attempted internationalism). While it is true that the democracies and communism attempt to spread their doctrine into every nation, one must ask whether or not this is the nature of communism and democracies or whether this is only an historical accident. It is doubtful that it is necessary for internationalism to be a part of either of these, and it could probably be demonstrated that both have functioned at some time or other on a particularistic basis. That criticism might not be true, however, if one replaced the concept of communism with the specific type of communism known as Marxism, which of necessity is internationalistic.

Teilhard's evaluation of the democratic structure is not a simple yes or no. He believes that democracy is a stage where the forces which are at work in humanity are expressing themselves in a profound but confused way. [17] He does not believe that the wave of the future is in the hands of the masses but that

the world of tomorrow will be born out of the 'elected' group of those (arising from any direction in class, and confession in the human world) who will decide that there is something big waiting for us ahead, and give their life to reach it.[18]

This is consistent with his biological interpretation of the movement of society. Every member of a species does not simultaneously acquire advanced survival mechanisms, but only a few, and in them is the key to the future. The total species is not the key to the future. If one follows the pattern of nature, he would end up, as Teilhard does, with a limited faith in democracy.

Teilhard evaluates modern democracy as a "strangely contagious modern obsession" which expresses itself in the legendary attributes of "liberty, equality, and fraternity." He has to redefine these completely before he can use them.[19] Above all he believes that the dialectics of nature and history will bring about a synthesis out of the polarization of the democracies on one side and socialism on the other. This will preserve both the individual and society as they will reinforce one another.

TOTALITARIANISM

Totalitarianism has aroused great political fear in the twentieth century because of various fascist, socialist, and communist governments. Teilhard touches sensitive nerves when he insists on the need for socialization which will bring totalization out of centreity, convergence and planetization. One might argue that totalization could be very different from totalitarianism. While this may be logically true, they seem to be closely related in Teilhard's thinking.

Speaking from a monist point of view (and Teilhard appears to be a sociological monist), he speaks of totalitarianism this way: "Seen in this light the modern totalitarian regimes, whatever their initial defects, are neither heresies nor biological regressions: they are in line with the essential trend of 'cosmic' movement." [20] It appears that he means

that totalitarianism is an expression of totalization and is
one of the necessary steps toward reaching the Omega Point
(and the Omega Point sounds totalitarian even if it is spiritual). Later Teilhard discusses some of the historical exam-
ples of totalitarianism and gives his evaluation: "My answer
is that I do not think we are yet in a position to judge recent
totalitarian experiments fairly." He adds: "It is not the
principle of totalisation that is at fault but the clumsy and
incomplete way in which it has been applied." [21] This must
mean that totalitarianism itself is not evil but that it has
suffered from incompetence and the lack of time for it to be
perfected.

The methods of totalitarianism are usually a bloody,
roughshod aggressiveness which is repugnant to those of
democratic persuasion. Teilhard obviously reacts against that
and wants to insure "that human totalisation is brought about,
not by the pressure of external forces, but through the internal working of harmonisation and sympathy." [22] One cannot imagine that human nature, as now known, would ever
have the kind of harmony and sympathy which would be
conducive to totalization, so Teilhard also awaits a kind of
conversion of human nature such as Marxism would need
to bring in its classless society.

The real secret of Teilhard's totalization (or totalitarianism) is that it is headed toward the future and is not based
upon a past or present political economy. Teilhard criticizes
fascism on this point: "Fascism is obstinately determined to
conceive and to build the modern world in the dimensions of
a bygone age." [23] Teilhard applies that criticism to every form
of government which is not trying to bring in the future.

> It seems to me the time has come to make a clean break with
> the old stuff. Fascism, Communism, democracy, have ceased
> to have any real meaning. My own dream would be to see
> the best of humanity regrouped on a spiritual basis deter-
> mined by the following three aims: Universalism, Futurism
> and Personalism, and co-operating in whatever political and

economic movement should prove technically most able to safeguard those three aims.[24]

If Herbert Marcuse is correct, Teilhard may be more radical in his totalitarian approach than Marxism. Marcuse admits only that the "totalitarian character of the revolution is made necessary by the totalitarian character of the capitalist relations of production,"[25] suggesting that the Marxist revolution was historically conditioned and that its odiousness will pass away after the destruction of what he calls "the totalitarianism of capitalism."

Teilhard's system might be best described as *"toward* a Christian philosophy, science or theology." The implication is that it was only "toward" and did not arrive. On the other hand, Teilhard adds a new dimension which few Christian thinkers have been willing to deal with. He attempts a synthesis of all reality, divine and human, social and individual, political and religious. He also attempts to project this synthesis to its ultimate conclusion without using some magic formula to separate it from the forces at work in the present.

While his attempt is commendable, it is just here that Teilhard has his greatest problem. He does not give adequate principles for living in the immediate and interim period between the present and the ultimate future. Others have evaluated the present and have attempted to right society according to the structures of the present, although they are completely relativistic and have lost sight of any ultimate in the future. Teilhard has the ultimate of the future without a satisfactory way of moving there from the present. He leaves the way open to all kinds of tyranny without proper guidelines as to whether such tyranny will lead us into the future satisfactorily. His only suggestion is that we must have insight into the wave of the future. That is hardly a satisfactory answer to a generation given to empiricism. One must accept the possibility, however, that Teilhard might be right in that only by intuition is it possible to know truth.

Teilhard's works give both a warning and a hope for social philosophy in a Christian context. The warning is that if any part of society is sick, all society may die. Christianity cannot afford to enhance the religious and ignore the social. The hope that Teilhard gives is that Christianity may not be irrelevant to the world after all.

VII. Teilhard's View of the Future

The future has two phases, according to Teilhard—the immediate and the distant. By looking at the past one can understand better these two aspects of the future. As we have seen, at various times in the history of the universe, critical points or thresholds have appeared. Here, according to Teilhard, significant new realities have emerged, including life and the mind. The development of agriculture and the industrial revolution may also be seen as critical events.

THE IMMEDIATE FUTURE

The immediate future should be seen against the background of the long development of the past. Inasmuch as history is headed toward an ultimate unification, the present period is important in that it is moving us toward that goal. The growth of industrialization necessitates intensive communication between people and between nations. Industrialization also produces dependence of nation upon nation. This inner network of interdependence will help to bring a universality of thought and life to every part of the world. Teilhard sees it as an intensification of the process of complexification. He not only predicts an acceleration of the industrialization for all nations but is very hopeful and positive about it, because it should speed up the whole process whereby we might reach another critical threshold in the not too distant future. The whole process of industrialization which brings intense communication and interdependence is a part of what he calls "the planetisation" of humanity.

Teilhard believes that man is beginning to think more and more as one mankind and make decisions as mankind rather than as private citizens or individual nations. Joseph Kopp points out that

> every single nation on our planet was represented at the opening of the Geophysical Year in 1954. That must have been the first decision to have been made by humanity as a whole. Pierre Teilhard was triumphant. He called 1954 the Year One of the Noosphere.[1]

Some followers of Teilhard insist that the next twenty years may be among the most important in all of the history of the planet. They believe that industrialization is reaching such fever pitch that the processes of interiorization and ramification are beginning to have their effects in such a way that man may cross the next threshold very shortly.[2] Rather than bemoaning the loss of the simple life and the pastoral scenes of a sentimental past, man should recognize that each threshold brings a giant leap for mankind. Therefore we should look for and cooperate with the forces of the world so as to speed, however possible, the next great leap across the threshold.

THE DISTANT FUTURE

For Teilhard, the future has also a distant phase. He expects in the distant future a complete metamorphosis of man. Individual men will be the building blocks for the reality of Mankind. By Mankind he does not mean a generalization or an abstraction but a new concrete reality which will make its appearance on earth. This is connected with the idea that a new threshold will be crossed in the distant future which will give rise to Mankind.

Teilhard is very interested in eugenics. This should not be surprising since we have seen his emphasis upon an orthogenetic biology. However, he is not considering eugenics when he speaks about a new superman (*Le Surhomme*). And his superman is different from Nietzsche's superman. Nietzsche sees his superman (*Übermensch*) as a grand human being whose personal gifts and faculties are greater than those around him from whom he has evolved. Teilhard sees his superman as having the totality of the faculties which are among men as a whole. This is not a " 'progress by isolation,' " [3] but rather the result of the confluence of thought and the coalescence, interiorization, and ramification of the hominids (man). Teilhard's superman is not the destruction of the individual man. The individual man continues his personalization but it is a superpersonalization.

In the long distant future these fundamental changes will take place in the universe as well as in man. Because of the problem of entropy, the universe will finally become a dead place and be unfit for human habitation as we know humanity now. For man to survive, he must undergo this change, must cross the critical threshold where individual men become the building blocks for the humankind which will rise. At that time man will no longer be dependent upon the physical but will transcend it, and so will be able to survive the death of the universe.

One chapter in the book *Science and Christ* is called "Super-Humanity, Super-Christ, Super-Charity." [4] This chapter portrays the distant future which Teilhard has in mind. Just as there will arise the superman (superhumanity), there will also arise the super-Christ in which the cosmic Christ and the Omega Point become a reality in history. There will also come about, according to Teilhard's scheme, super-charity. This is the universalization of the love which humans know on individual levels now. This will become the underlying structure of the future universe.

Teilhard uses broad strokes to paint the picture of the history of the universe. He is unlike most historians, who begin the story of man and his culture with the earliest and most primitive civilizations and end with an empirical view of the present generation. Teilhard goes back before man to the pre-hominid forms of life—and actually before that to the pre-life history of the world. He sees a thread, a direction, which runs through all of the critical thresholds before the appearance of man on past empirical history into the future. Teilhard feels that it is erroneous to take merely the brief history of mankind and view it so positivistically that one cannot see the pattern and direction of human development.

THE FUTURE HAS A GOAL

One idea is fundamental to all of Teilhard's thought—that the future has a goal. History is not merely a meandering. Whatever nondirection seems to be there is only because man is caught in such circumstances that he gives his attention to the immediate rather than to the whole perspective of history. For Teilhard, history is going somewhere.

The idea that the future has a goal is a part of Teilhard's evolutionary theory. Many evolutionists, however, have disagreed with Teilhard's position or have refused to commit themselves because of differences in evolutionary theories.

In order to see the situation it is necessary to put the history of evolutionary theory into some perspective. Evolutionary theory is not a recent development in spite of the fact that its influence has only recently reached such great proportions. As early as the Greek philosopher Empedocles (5th c. B.C.), there was an emphasis upon the eternal becoming which Empedocles applied to biological and cosmological functions.[5] It was Aristotle in the following century who gave

Greek philosophy a strong sense of the dynamic with his belief that everything was moving from potentiality to actuality. The principle of entelechy was the inner force directing everything toward its goal. Aristotle's entelechy is not unlike Teilhard's radial energy. However, early in the Christian era and particularly in the Middle Ages, a static concept of the world developed, perhaps mainly out of the theological understanding of the Hebrew-Christian idea of instantaneous creationism by God. This view held constant into the nineteenth century, although there were dissenting voices here and there. In Immanuel Kant (18th c.) for instance, there is the idea of progressive development of the human race.

One of the first big steps in evolutionary theory was the publication of the French naturalist, Jean Lamarck's *Philosophie Zoologique* in 1809. Lamarck suggested evolution through acquired characteristics. However, the time for the idea of evolution to be accepted had not yet come. Such men as George Cuvier, a contemporary of Lamarck, opposed his evolutionary theory and helped to continue the climate which was unfavorable to the acceptance of Lamarck's view.

Two philosophers contributed much to the acceptance of evolutionary theory. Not that they were biological evolutionists but their philosophies were dynamic rather than static. These philosophers were Georg W. F. Hegel (1770–1830) with his dialectical method and Auguste Comte (1798–1857) with his three stages of human thought. The work which these men did in the nineteenth century laid the groundwork for acceptance of a dynamic view of human progression. It was against this background that Darwin published his *Origin of Species* in 1859. Now the time was ripe, and his theories found immediate acceptance in the world of science.

It is precisely here, however, that the evolutionary theory of Teilhard meets with resistance. Darwin and his followers spoke about blind chance being at the root of the evolutionary process. But as we have seen, Teilhard believed that there is direction to the evolutionary process (orthogenesis), and when the proper conditions are reached, something new appears which has not been present before. This has often been interpreted as spontaneous generation. For example, life appeared when certain molecules came to their proper relationship under proper conditions. Darwinianism has always opposed spontaneous generation. Followers of Darwin have implied that Teilhard's position was rejected in the ideas of Lamarck, and evolution only became acceptable when Lamarck was corrected by Darwin. There is some question, however, as to whether Darwin's success was due to his more appropriate idea or because of the historical conditions which prevailed at the time that he offered his evolutionary theory. This latter view was the historical interpretation of Bernard Delfgaauw.[6]

Orthogenesis is essential to Teilhard's understanding of the evolutionary process. It too has a parallel in Aristotle's principle of entelechy. Orthogenesis is the variations found in organisms through successive generations which come about because of the predetermination of "withinness" and result in progress. Teilhard believes that this is a declaration of purpose. He describes orthogenesis as a kind of groping.

> This groping strangely combines the blind fantasy of large numbers with the precise orientation of a specific target. It would be a mistake to see it as mere chance. Groping is *directed chance*.[7]

Teilhard believes that there is a guiding thread running through the whole of history and reality which necessitates the interpretation of directedness—that is, the development of the nervous system and then consciousness. Because of this coherence it is possible to see that there is a direction in evolution.[8]

Teilhard's thesis has divided the scientific world. There are scientists who assert the nonscientific character of Teilhard's work and look upon him as primarily a theologian or mystic. Others, such as Theodosius Dobzhansky, believe that

Teilhard has made a significant contribution to science whether or not scientists are willing to accept all of his theories.

One area which Teilhard insists the scientific world needs to deal with is the "within" of things. P. G. Fothergill says of Teilhard,

> He struggled hard to convince his fellow scientists that it is urgently necessary for them to consider consciousness as an integral part of things, that is, to consider the 'within' on equal terms with the 'without.' [9]

Shortly before his death Teilhard prepared a paper in defense of orthogenesis, attempting to put orthogenesis on a scientific basis rather than the mysticism he was accused of. He says:

> No 'mysticism' (whatever my friend M. W. Wood may say) is implied in the recognition of this phenomenon which inevitably reminds us of the entirely material phenomenon of a river gradually establishing its course to conform with the terrain over which it flows. [10]

Teilhard does not attempt to do away with all of the mechanisms which biological science has found in its study of evolutionary process. Instead he superimposes his idea of orthogenesis upon the orthodox causal explanations of evolution. By the withinness of things, the processes of orthodox Darwinian biology are directed.

The idea of progress has had a checkered history. With the Renaissance, a new optimism was born with the possibility of attaining the golden age. This optimism was heightened during the nineteenth century. The philosophies of Hegel, Nietzsche, Marx and Engels contributed to this, no doubt. But while the Western world believed that there would be social progress, there were no similar hopes for the biological progress of man, in spite of the doctrine of evolution. The First World War shattered the dreams of man's social progress, leaving the view of man's future either neutral or pessimistic both in the social and the biological areas of

interpretation. Teilhard turns all of this around in his
thought. He was one of the first to say that man has a positive
biological future. Evolution is not static nor has it reached
its greatest height, but it has great possibilities for the future
development of the human race. At the same time, Teilhard
has a great optimism about the social future of man. This
is possible because he does not divide the biological and
social as was done in Cartesian dualism. Rather he sees the
principles of centration which are at work in the social arena
also at work at the biological level.

Teilhard sees the pattern of evolution as being irreversible.
While there are palaeontologists who believe that if the human branch perished through self-destruction or some other
catastrophe, the cosmos would put forth another human
branch, Teilhard does not. There was only one time in the
history of the world that the conditions were just right for
the creation of the human species. Those conditions can never
be expected again.

The progress which has resulted from the action of orthogenesis cannot be seen by looking at a few years of human
history. The whole of human history over the many millennia
must be considered.

Teilhard begins one of his essays by saying:

> By 'faith in Man' we mean here the more or less active
> and fervent conviction that Mankind as an organic and
> organised whole possesses a future: a future consisting not
> merely of successive years but of higher states to be achieved
> by struggle. Not merely survival, let us be clear, but some
> form of higher life or super-life.[11]

It is not always easy to perceive the movement of progress;
"the larger a thing is, the slower is its movement." [12] The
hugeness of the universe of course means that it is more
difficult to chart the course of progress but it is there. Nevertheless, he says:

Research shows that from the lowest to the highest level of the organic world there is a persistent and clearly defined thrust of animal forms towards species with more sensitive and elaborate nervous systems.[13]

In spite of the fact that our universe was created several billion years ago, "Our modern world was created in less than 10,000 years, and in the past 200 years it has changed more than in all the preceding millennia."[14]

The future has a goal. It is not heading up a blind alley. Teilhard sees the whole process of evolution as a process in which there is progress.

THE TRANSFORMATION OF THE UNIVERSE

The Coming Transformation

Teilhard believes that there is coming a grand transformation of the universe which will be a great final mystery. Individual men will become Mankind which will be a superhumanity. This is another way of talking about the personalized universe which will come about when the elements of personhood grow more intense, approaching the consummation of the universe when there will no longer be man and nature, separated, but one superhuman person.

The transformation will also include what Teilhard calls the super-Christ.

By Super-Christ, I most certainly do not mean *another* Christ, a second Christ different from and greater than the first. I mean *the same* Christ, the Christ of all time, revealing himself to us in a form and in dimensions, with an urgency and area of contact, that are enlarged and given new force.[15]

He later says: "Christ coincides (though this assertion will have to be examined more deeply) with what I earlier called Omega Point."[16] At the time in which this happens, Christ

will have become a complete part of the human consciousness and the dominant force of the superhumanity which will
have appeared.

The third area of transformation is super-charity, which
will be the universalization of the love man has already experienced. However, it will not just be man's love suddenly
expanding to a universal scope, but it will be the synthesis
of all the love of all men in the superhumanity through the
super-Christ. The super-charity will be the ultimate of the
interior life and withinness. At that point human relationships
will no longer be external bodily relationships with another
person, but will be of a "psychical character of a centre-to-
centre relationship, in other words, an act of love." [17]

This coming transformation will no doubt take place
through the result of changing conditions in the planet earth.
However, as has been true in the other unique changes which
have come about, the earth's conditions will reach a critical
point at which in a sudden moment this transfiguration will
take place, and the earth will be changed from a more or
less Cartesian dualism to one personalized universe.

The Mechanisms of Transformation

Evolution is the most obvious mechanism of transformation. As we have seen Teilhard is dedicated to a kind of
transformism whereby the species are not fixed but are transformed into new emergents.

Part of the evolutionary process is the mechanism of
convergence and centration. The infrastructure of reality is
such that it will bring about the convergence of all things.
"Everything that rises must converge." [18] A peduncle develops phyla because there is dispersal and diversity at the level
of the peduncle, but then there comes the beginning of convergence to a single phylum. Out of that phylum comes another peduncle which means another divergence. This is the
process which our universe has experienced since its beginning. Sometimes Teilhard refers to this process as unan-

imisation.[19] It is a basic presupposition of Teilhard that the principle of centration is at work in the universe and, regardless of the divergence of species and reality at a given moment, all will finally come to a place of convergence. The ultimate convergence is the final Omega Point.

Another part of the process is the mechanism of totalization and planetization. These are words Teilhard uses to express the idea that personalization, hominisation and love will totally absorb the planet. What Teilhard describes cannot happen to a few people who will become the supermen over all the others. Rather there must be that critical moment when the whole universe will be transformed. But first, the conditions which would bring about this transformation must become widespread. As we have already seen, there must develop the planetization of communications, industrialization, and population. But also the principles of love, withinness, and radial energy must become intense not only within a few men but within the whole universe. The time must come when physical communion, economic interdependence, and face-to-face contact have spread to all men everywhere. This is planetization.

Another mechanism of transformation is love. Teilhard is willing to admit that love is the emotional reaction between persons, but he feels it is much more real than this. He often speaks of love as an energy within the psychic universe. It seems as though he means that love is not just an emotional reaction and sentimentality but is also a full biological reality of affinity of being to being which reaches down below the level of the human.

> Considered in its full biological reality, love—that is to say, the affinity of being with being—is not peculiar to man. It is a general property of all life and as such it embraces, in its varieties and degrees, all the forms successively adopted by organised matter. In the mammals, so close to ourselves, it is easily recognized in its different modalities: sexual passion, parental instinct, social solidarity, etc. Farther off, that is to

say lower down on the tree of life, analogies are more obscure until they become so faint as to be imperceptible. But this is the place to repeat what I said earlier when we were discussing the '*within* of things.' If there were no internal propensity to unite, even at a prodigiously rudimentary level—indeed in the molecule itself—it would be physically impossible for love to appear higher up, with us, in 'hominised' form.[20]

Here his thought reaches the full cycle. It is love which is the energy that has brought about the attraction or affinity of realities to one another, which in turn is the power of centration and convergence.

Christopher Mooney makes an interesting statement at this point. He has been discussing Teilhard's view of the church and goes on to say,

This brief backward glance at Teilhard's early references to the Church will serve as background for the concept which he is now about to propose, namely that this Christian 'axis' is in reality a 'phylum of love' inserted by God into the evolutionary process.[21]

If Mooney is correct in his interpretation, the church is where the intensity of love is at the present time. It is the phylum out of which will come the personalized universe, and therefore the superhumanity, super-Christ and super-charity.

The Product of the Transformation—The Noosphere

The noosphere is that envelope of mind and reflective thought which spreads over the surface of the world superimposed upon the biosphere. It is the distinctive element of significance in mankind. Noogenesis is both the birth and the developmental process of the noosphere. The noosphere has developed out of the noogenesis especially of the primates which came through their increasing cerebralization. Teilhard described this layer of mind about the earth as the "phosphorescence of thought." [22] The noosphere was able to develop because of the development of the hominids, that is, man. The pre-hominids did not have the cerebral capacity for a brain large enough to develop sufficiently for modern man (see chapter V). But when the hominid stage was reached, with an increased cranial capacity, mind could develop, and the intensifying process of noogenesis could continue.[23]

As the population of the earth grows, there are more and more islands of intelligence scattered throughout the world. These tend to converge through communications and the interdependence of our technological and industrial world. One result is the intensification of research. Technology and industrialization are creating the desire for research, and the leisure produced by technology enables certain individuals and groups to perform the research. The increased research has intensified the cerebralization of the human mind, is heating it up, so to speak, making complexification even more pronounced and effective. This means that man is headed more and more toward the period of time when the conditions will be right for the step into the personalized universe.[24]

The noosphere comes from the growth process of mind which brings about progressive intensification. Teilhard sees all of this coalescence developing through the common efforts of science, art, ethics and religion. This is a picture of movement from the individual to the social and from the multiple to unity.

The social aspect is very important here. Apparently the basic capacity of man now is no greater than it was in Cro-Magnon Man. Then why is it that presently man is so much farther advanced in technology and knowledge than Cro-Magnon Man? The only answer is that progress is social. Teilhard speaks of the effectiveness of the "collective memory of the human race," and "the heredity of example and education." [25]

The complexification developing over the world brings about an increased noogenesis, a rise in consciousness.

> No one can deny that a network (a world network) of economic and psychic affiliations is being woven at ever increasing speed which envelops and constantly penetrates more deeply within each of us. With every day that passes it becomes a little more impossible for us to act or think otherwise than collectively.[26]

He wants to canalize this rising tide of consciousness, intensifying the phenomenon of research, producing a transformation which would be increasingly mental.

What is happening in the noogenesis process is a continuing development of this world network which he calls the collective megasynthesis—an independent integrated network. Individual decisions can be made, but there is such an interdependence and a massive network of communications that minds must act in unison to achieve their purposes. There is something of a collective cloud of minds which is coalescing and speeding up the evolutionary process.

One may look for a new step in this whole process when the world moves beyond the collective to the highly personal, the hyperpersonal. Here, the world will be personalized, the personalized universe will have arrived. However, at this point, Teilhard warns against impatience at the sight of modern man in dissension with himself.

> Similarly, and despite an almost explosive acceleration of noogenesis at our level, we cannot expect to see the earth transform itself under our eyes in the space of a generation. Let us keep calm and take heart.[27]

In spite of that warning, Teilhard encourages us to look for a breakthrough in the process of hominisation. The process of socialization will go on, and there will continue to be even more psychic inner connections.

THE OMEGA POINT

As Teilhard looks at the history of the world, he sees the pattern of diversification to unification repeated again and again—into the future. As far as man is concerned, from the first men have developed hunting groups, then agricultural groups, and today the vast, diversified economic and psychic networks which, although divided into East and West, will someday coalesce and develop a pan-organized world. The final result of this will be the personalized universe.

For Teilhard this is a result of the principle of centreity which operates on all phenomena so that as species evolve, they curve in from diversity toward a unity at the center. Teilhard sees the world as having burst forth from one primal peduncle into a myriad of forms and further peduncles which now are all beginning to move back toward a single point. This is not the primal point but the Omega Point. The Omega Point is the apex of all of nature, the end of the historical process. The Omega Point is not just a collection of all of the things which have preceded it in nature and history but contains an emergent new order.

Teilhard describes the Omega Point as being hyper-personal and identifies it from time to time with the Christosphere or the cosmic Christ. Beyond this he gives at least four attributes of the Omega Point.[28] The first is *autonomy*. The physical earth, as it is now, faces death especially because of the operation of the law of entropy. The time will come when the universe no longer has any available energy. Teilhard recognizes this fact of science, even though he does hint that inasmuch as entropy affects only tangential energy, it may be that radial energy renews the supply of tangential energy. Nevertheless, the basic position of Teilhard is that the earth will die as a result of entropy. Therefore the Omega Point must be autonomous from the superstructure of the earth in order for it to survive the death of the earth. As he put it, "Omega must be independent of the collapse of the forces with which evolution is woven." [29]

Actuality is another attribute of the Omega Point. Teilhard believes in emergence in evolution. What arises out of evolution is not just a combination of things but a new reality. That is, there emerges a new ontological actuality which was not in existence before. Out of the womb of the evolutionary process there will be born from the physical threshold a new entity or actuality.

Irreversibility is an important attribute of the Omega Point. History itself is irreversible, so that you cannot go back and redo it. Once that reality, entity, or actuality has crossed the threshold, something irreversible has happened. That entity has appeared because its time has come, the right set of conditions came together only at that one time. Therefore, the production of the entity can never be repeated. Nor can there be a step back through the threshold, in order to become less than the entity it now is. So in the future, the whole process of the Omega Point is irreversible. Once it has been reached, it becomes the ultimate new entity in the universe.

The Omega also has the attribute of *transcendence*. Transcendence occurs whenever a new entity arises out of an old attribute or reality. When molecules combine to form a cell, the cell in some way transcends the attributes and characteristics of the molecules which form it. It is something different from and more than those molecules. So when the Omega Point is reached, it will not be just the universe carried to a more complex degree, but will be a reality which transcends the building blocks which compose it.

The principle of convergence, which has been an important characteristic in Teilhard's thought, is very evident here. Everything is moving from Alpha to Omega. Omega is the final outcome of economic interdependence, communion among political groups, communications network, the dense populations of the earth, the coalescence of science and religion, and even the ecumenics of the moving together of the religious world. Until about twenty thousand years ago, all of the forms of nature seemed to be spreading, diversifying and multiplying. However, the past 20,000 years has marked the beginning of convergence and unification.

THE CHRISTOSPHERE

Teilhard's reference to the super-Christ may sound strange to ears accustomed to traditional religious terminology. Teilhard understands that "in position and function, Christ, here and now, fills for us the place of Omega Point." [30] This super-Christ, who is the Omega Point, is the final point whether you arrive from theology or anthropology. The two coincide or at least overlap. It is Christ who fills all things. Here Teilhard appeals to St. Paul, especially to his letters to the Ephesians and the Colossians (Col. 1:17, 2:10, 3:11; Eph. 4:9). It is Christ who consummates all things, and who gives meaning and coherence to the structural lines of the world which converge upon him.

Whenever Teilhard speaks about the other spheres (biosphere, noosphere, etc.), he speaks of a layer which surrounds the earth. There is some question whether that image holds true of the Christosphere or not. Sometimes it sounds more as if the Christ is a part of the infrastructure of the world rather than a layer of reality surrounding the earth. At other times it appears as though the Christ is the energy which pervades the universe. Once Teilhard commented that "Christ is linked, not simply in a moral or juridical context but as it were structurally and organically with the cosmos." [31] Another time he indicated "that Christ is the great source of power and energy which is drawing all things toward itself." [32]

The historic Jesus of Nazareth is not often mentioned in the writings of Teilhard. This is not the denial of Jesus but is perhaps his taking for granted the historic Christian tradition. In referring to super-Christ Teilhard does not mean *another* Christ, or a second Christ who is different or greater than the first Christ. He does see the super-Christ as being the One who is at the end of the process of evolution. As he puts it, "The total Christ is consummated and may be attained only at the term of universal evolution." [33] It may be

true that Teilhard does not believe that the Christ and the
super-Christ are different, but it is also obvious that the
"noogenesis is consummated in a Christogenesis." [34]

The Christ of the Christosphere is a universal and cosmic
Christ. Teilhard says: "By the Universal Christ, I mean
Christ the organic centre of the entire universe." [35] This is
the Christ who is the infrastructure of the world. He is also
the cosmic Christ because he is the Christ of the entire universe and cosmic system. This is not a static kind of pantheism such as many monists hold. Teilhard differentiates his
view from others', saying that

> unlike the false monisms which urge one through passivity
> into unconsciousness, the 'pan-Christism' which I am discov-
> ering places union at the term of an arduous process of
> differentiation.[36]

This cosmic Christ is not one who is the result of imagination
or theologizing, but is the product of the long historical
process of the universe.

Teilhard sees the church as the body of Christ, not merely
in a mystical sense but in a much more realistic sense. The
individuals of the church are the building blocks of the body
of Christ or the Christosphere just as molecules are the
building blocks of the physical universe. A love which is the
major attribute of the Christ can only be expressed ade-
quately through the individuals who are here in the universe.
(Cf. Mooney's term for the church, the "phylum of love." [37])
Teilhard is not interested in narrowing the body of Christ
to a particular confessional group. He believes that there is
developing a convergence of all religions, a drawing to a
convergent Omega Point in all of the universe.[38] There is a
way in which the whole universe is the body of Christ, but
the church is that specially selected instrument which knows
the way the future is going (eschatology) and which therefore has the ability to lead in being both the body of Christ
and the vehicle of super-charity.

All of this is possible because there is a movement toward unity. All things will be united in Christ in the universe. While this force is working upon religions so that they will be converging, it is also at work at every level of the universe. Joseph Kopp has pointed out that: "According to Teilhard we are going to leave the age of *religions* and enter the age of *Religion*." [39] All things are going to come to their climactic head in Jesus Christ who will be the summation of all the forces of the universe. Teilhard describes this with such words as *hyperpersonal*. All is caught up in Christ after it has crossed the critical threshold and has moved into the Christosphere.

Salvation is bound together with this whole process. Teilhard does not discuss the salvation of individual men but discusses salvation in terms of the race reaching the Omega Point. Kopp interprets it this way: "God-made-Man Christ is simultaneously the axis and final goal of salvation." [40] It is the universal and cosmic Christ who is the final goal of salvation. The final step will be at the universalization of all things and the crossing of the critical threshold into the Christosphere.

MAN'S PLACE TODAY—COOPERATION

While the future development of the world is dependent upon the radial energy which is moving toward the cosmic Christ, there are ways in which the human family can speed up the process of noogenesis toward the Christosphere. Since the world must move toward convergence, it is obvious that any ideas of isolation and hyperindividualism would be counterproductive and therefore impede that movement. Rather the human family should be seeking a collectivism and an interdependence among itself. This will entail at least two things: universality and unity. The universality will be achieved when man attempts to understand values in a cosmic way.

The unity will occur when man tries to bring all together not simply as an aggregation but to wait for the aggregation to be made into the hyperpersonal.

Believing that the world is heading toward the Omega Point and that this development is irreversible carries with it a significant determinism. Yet, Teilhard does not wish to deny the reality of human freedom. However, that freedom is a freedom to cooperate with the evolutionary process to help move it on toward its goal.

There are many ways by which man can cooperate with the forces at work around him. Perhaps one of the most obvious ones is through research. As research goes on, it brings about an intensification of the noogenesis process, developing mind. It is almost that mind heats up until it finally reaches the boiling point where there is a transformation from one form to another. It is that transformation that the evolutionary process is seeking as it moves man on and on toward the goal of superhumanization.

N. M. Wildiers commented at this point:

> Teilhard never envisaged the future of evolution of man as an ineluctable necessity in which human freedom would have no part to play at all. On the contrary, . . . he calls most emphatically for man's collaboration in the process of completing cosmic evolution and sees this free collaboration as an essential factor in the course of events. We are to understand his predictions, then, as having not a deterministic but only a statistical character.[41]

Wildiers is correct in his evaluation that human freedom plays a significant part as man collaborates with the process of cosmic evolution. But Teilhard is not the positivist who uses only statistical probability. While he traces the evolution of man from the beginning into the dim, distant future, he does not give a scientific, statistical analysis in a sense of positivistic natural science or sociology. Unlike the positivists, Teilhard sees that process and progress are grounded in the very nature and structure of the world.

VIII. Teilhard's Purpose

One can discern three main purposes in the writings of
Teilhard de Chardin, although he may not have always held
them consciously before him as he wrote. They are faithfulness to conscience, apologetics and science.

FAITHFULNESS TO CONSCIENCE

Teilhard de Chardin had a strong sense of conscience which
was a characteristic of the people from Auvergne from
which he came. Henri de Lubac, in his introduction to the
Letters to Leontine Zanta, quotes Teilhard as follows:

> They want me to promise in writing that I will never *say*
> or write anything against the traditional position of the
> Church on original sin. Hence, anguish of conscience:

> It's both too vague and too absolute. I feel I should, in
> conscience, reserve for myself (1) the right to carry on
> research with professional men (*ex Jure naturali*); (2)
> the right to bring help to the disturbed and troubled (*ex
> Jure sacerdotali*). I'm hoping to be able to get the formula
> they are asking me to sign altered into something of this
> kind: 'I bind myself not to spread (not to carry on
> proselytism for) the particular explanations contained in
> my notes.'[1]

Teilhard's conscience was aimed toward the Divine and not toward satisfying human and social demands. He understood that above all he must fulfill the will of God in his life. He was certain that the will of God for him, for the church and for the world were all the same. At least he did not believe that his will was what the world ought to do but that he and the world were struggling together to find and fulfill the will of God. Obviously he felt that if he was fulfilling the will of God, there was no real reason for apprehension. He once wrote to his cousin:

> About your own personal concerns—listen once more while I repeat what is one of my firmest convictions, as your cousin and as a priest: 'Don't worry about whether your life is worthwhile, about its anomalies, its disappointments, its somewhat obscure and somber future. You are doing what God wills. In the midst of your anxieties and dissatisfactions you are offering him the sacrifice of a humble soul bowing, in spite of everything, to an austere Providence.' [2]

Teilhard went on to admit that such expression in fulfilling God's will might not be the most enjoyable but was certainly the most important.

Faithfulness of conscience meant also a faithfulness to Christ. Many times Teilhard expressed his mystical communion with Christ and his love for Christ—the universal Christ who is the fulfillment of all men in history. He was more concerned with the universal Christ than the Jesus of the past because he saw that Christ is the future toward which God is moving all things. If one were disloyal to Christ, he would be disloyal to the future. Therefore, loyalty to God, Christ and the future were all part of the same cloth of his conscience. Many Christians feel in their consciences that they must remain loyal to tradition, but Teilhard had the same steadfastness about the future. He did not turn his back upon tradition, however, and found it

exceedingly important. But its importance had to be measured in the light of the future. Any tradition which got in
the way of the future had to be resisted. Teilhard felt he
owed a debt to the past but a greater debt to the future.
The church was part of the conscience of Teilhard inasmuch as he was a son of the church and in her service. He
saw the church as the community of the universal Christ.
However, he came into conflict with his superiors in the
church in what Robert Speaight calls "the crisis of obedi-
ence." [3] Teilhard's conflict with the church was very frustrating to him, and he died without seeing his manuscripts in
print. He certainly had many occasions to publish his
material through his many friends outside the clergy and his
association with the Wenner Gren Foundation, a private
foundation who sponsored Teilhard's research in the last
months of his life. While he certainly felt pressure from
his ecclesiastical superiors, only his strong sense of conscience toward the church prevented publication. He never
turned his back on his church nor did he bring bitter public
attacks against her.

Teilhard's difficulties did not leave him unscarred. He
once wrote to Père Valensin:

> Dear Friend, please help me. I've put a good face on it
> outwardly, but within it is something that resembles an agony
> or a storm. I think I see that, if I separated myself off, or
> kicked over the traces in any way whatsoever (humanly
> speaking, it would be so simple and so 'easy'), I would be
> disloyal to my faith in our Lord's animation of everything
> that happens, and in his own value, superior to that of all
> the elements of this world. Moreover I would be compromis-
> ing . . . the religious value of my ideas. People would see
> it as turning my back on the Church, as pride, who knows
> what? It is essential that I should show, by my example, that
> if my ideas seem innovations, they nevertheless make me as
> faithful as anyone to the old attitude. That's what I think I
> see. But even here, there are shadows. . . .[4]

APOLOGETICS

Teilhard cannot be understood unless he is seen as an apologist. Some interpreters suggest that one reason for the difficulties Teilhard had with church officials was that they did not understand that he was attempting an apologetic task, not writing dogmatics. Once, after describing what he understood faith to be, Teilhard commented:

> I know no other apologetics for my own self: and I cannot therefore suggest any other to those for whom I wish the supreme happiness of one day finding themselves face to face with a unified universe.[5]

Apologetics was a natural task for Teilhard because he was trained in theology and philosophy and was a devout man of the church. In addition, his scientific training put him in a unique position to be an apologist to leaders of scientific thought and those influenced by science. Claude Cuenot appraises the situation this way:

> The whole of Teilhard's spirituality and especially *Le Milieu Divin*, is addressed to: (1) Christians whose spirituality is too narrow, who divorce the spiritual too much from terrestrial. . . . (2) believers who hesitate to enter the Church from fear of loving the earth too much.[6]

Apologetics must deal with the problems of suffering and theodicy (justifying the righteousness of God). In his apologetic task, Teilhard discussed these subjects, sometimes pointedly and at other times by implication. His basic approach was to point out the necessity of suffering in an evolving world and the future grand design toward which God is moving the world.

One of Teilhard's most important tasks was the integration of science and faith. He wanted to show that these were both legitimate parts of truth—the outer and the inner. This integration was not simply the coalescing of science and religion, but involved the spiritual and the material, the personal and the nonpersonal, the empirical and the intuitive.

Wildiers described Teilhard's apologetic task as trying to square the natural sciences (the world) with the inner reality (the divine). Teilhard tried to make the spiritual believable to those who were empiricists.

For Teilhard, his apologetic task was a challenging one. He recognized the need for theological correctives and was willing to rework his apologetic propositions within certain limits. However, he did not feel constrained to be bound by the language of traditional theology in his apologetic task.

SCIENCE

Teilhard stated his specific task as "the right to carry on research with professional men (*ex Jure naturali*)." [7]

From his earliest years his bent was toward science. One of Teilhard's earliest co-workers, Henri Bremond, said about Teilhard that "he had another passion, a jealous, absorbing passion, that made him live in a different world from ours: he was in love with stones." [8] Abbé Grenet later spoke of two characteristics which made Teilhard a great scientist—his exceptional scientific knowledge and his ability to see everything. [9] Teilhard left behind a vast amount of technical literature for scientists. Claude Cuenot has developed a bibliography of these works which is nearly forty pages of small print. [10]

As was true of many who shared his visions in science, Teilhard was eager, enthusiastic and compulsive about his scientific work. In the course of his work he traveled in the continents of Europe, Asia, Africa, North America, South America and Australia and in the subcontinental areas of India and Indonesia.

Teilhard's most important book, *The Phenomenon of Man*, combines the two purposes of apologetics and science. He built a whole system of evolution from his special phenomenological point of view, which included natural science and observation about the design he saw in evolution. Examining the evidence of man's arrival in the world he went on to show an inner purpose behind it all, a psychic world as well as a physical world. His biological theory was radically different from Darwin's but his "new science" was necessary for his apologetic program.

It was natural for Teilhard to combine the vocations of Christian apologetics and science because he saw that there is one God of revelation and the world. This God is the inner drive of all that has happened and is happening. Theology and science are two aspects of one study which need to be synthesized.

IX. Teilhard's Presuppositions and Methods

PRESUPPOSITIONS

The statement of belief with which Teilhard begins his book *How I Believe* is one of the clearest statements of his beliefs and presuppositions.[1] (See above, chap. I, the section on "Teilhard's Faith.")

Teilhard's statement of his presuppositions must be taken seriously. He was a man who was highly introspective and given to self-examination about motives and work. But no matter how great a genius or how thoroughly introspective, can any man truly step outside of himself and gauge the inward forces at work within him? Therefore it is necessary to examine Teilhard's writings for presuppositions which may also include driving forces behind the presuppositions of which he was aware.

It will not always be possible to separate his presuppositions from his methods. Some of the structures of reality mentioned earlier may not be presuppositions as much as some named in this chapter. Nevertheless, proceeding on the hope of clarifying several issues, several presuppositions will be named in this chapter.

God

Teilhard's foremost presupposition is the reality of God. His family's piety as well as his faith, his early training, his

Catholic vows, his Jesuit membership, all created within Teilhard a faith in the Divine which he could not forsake. Certainly it came out differently than it did in some of his fellow Romanists and Jesuits. Sometimes his idea of God seems intensely personal; at other times it seems pantheistic, as though God were the impersonal force spread throughout the universe; and at times it is closely akin to the God of the process philosophers. Nevertheless, however he defined God, Teilhard faced every kind of knowledge by relating it to the Divine.

Teilhard uses many names to express his idea of God, some of them not usually associated with the Divine—the One, the All in All, Love, Energy, the Within, Omega and Spirit. God for Teilhard is the Director at the intersection of every event in the universe. His God is the energizing force of every action. This interpretation means that God is the thread which makes up the fabric of Teilhard's thought.

Complexity

A second presupposition is that the complex is better than the simple. One might take this for granted in the modern world filled with sophisticated machinery. However the history of philosophy has a long tradition of honoring the simple rather than the complex, following Aristotle, who believed that all things were moving toward the final state of motionlessness. Motion was caused by incomplete and imperfect entities striving for the state of completion and perfection. All things were moving from diversity to a simplicity, and when they arrived motion would cease.

Christian theology has also spoken of the *simplicitas dei*— the simplicity of God—as describing the real God of the Judaeo-Christian tradition. That is, God is pure being, of one substance as the creed puts it, rather than a confusion of parts and complexities. Judaism especially stressed the oneness of the godhead to counteract the doctrine of the Trinity.

On another level, Teilhard's fellow Frenchman, Jean

Jacques Rousseau, glorified the simple and primitive life. Although he was not naïve enough to think that he could return to the primitive life, he saw it as the good life. As a result the least interference by government and schools was preferable. The "natural self" was the condition to be desired rather than artificially imposing upon people complexities and niceties.

Teilhard swims against this stream believing that complexity is to be desired rather than simplicity. Complexity is the result of the growth of the human spirit and of energy turned in upon itself. While Teilhard speaks about oneness in unity, his oneness is not that of simplicity but of a complexity which becomes so intense that it transcends the various parts to become a new "whole" incorporating the totality of the complex parts. This presupposition of complexity is important to Teilhard because it is the force of the movement of evolution, orthogenesis, and the whole idea of superpersonality such as noosphere and Christosphere.

Purpose

A major presupposition of Teilhard is the reality of orthogenesis, which indicates that there is purpose in what is happening in the world. While this purpose is more easily identified in hominisation, Teilhard traces it through the whole history of the phenomenon of the world since creation. To be sure this presupposition is related to the previous presuppositions (God and complexity). However, a Darwinian might admit that the complex is better than the simple without ever discussing purposiveness in the evolutionary process. Also one might think of God in some deistic or pantheistic fashion without relating him to the movement of the universe toward a goal. Every page of Teilhard's writings carries the burden of showing purpose working itself out in the minutia of events, whether those events are physical or mental. He seeks to show that over the whole course of the history of the universe that there is no other way to explain what has happened other than to attribute purpose to the process. This means the inevitability of progress until the ultimate goal of orthogenesis is reached.

Unity

The oneness and unity of all things is another basic presupposition. One of the fundamental issues in Teilhard's thought is the relationship of the one and the many.[2] Teilhard does not see this as a problem but understands that there is an underlying unity behind all things, even in the apparent diversity. All things are moving toward a unity, though they must go through diverse stages. Although Teilhard recognizes that there is an inner and an outer to reality, that there is the physical as well as the mental, he also believes in the coalescence of all things and the fundamental unity behind both matter and energy.

Nonreversibility

A fundamental presupposition of Teilhard is the idea of nonreversibility. When a threshold (or point of intensity) is crossed and a new level of reality is reached, there can never be a crossing back over that threshold again so that the new entity would disappear. In other words, when there has been a fundamental change in the structure of reality and the picture of progress, there can be no reversal of that procedure. While there may be variations within the new stage that is reached, that stage can never disappear.

This is a presupposition which many do not share. Many have taught that there could be fundamental regression as well as disintegration of values attained. In other words, if there can be evolution towards the more complex and adaptable, there can also be evolution which would be opposite the values generally held for a species. However, Teilhard's system is nonreversible. In his dialectical scheme, after there has been a movement across one threshold, varying qualities of complexity and value may develop prior to the crossing of a second threshold, but the original threshold cannot be crossed again by the universe.

Institutionalism

Another presupposition on which Teilhard operated has been overlooked by interpreters—that is, his faith in institutions. Despite the difficulties he had with the Roman Catholic church and the Jesuits, he never lost his faith in the ultimate triumph of truth and the institution. This may be explained in part from his family background of people identified with the nobility. His view of the future is that of a superorganization which becomes so intricate and complex, so sophisticated and interwoven, that it crosses a threshold transcending itself so that the superorganization becomes supermind. The question is whether or not his faith in institutions leads him to project this crossing of a new threshold. Or perhaps he arrives at the idea of a supermind and applies his basic feelings for institutions to supply the answer as to how that supermind will be created.

This is not to say that Teilhard was not aware of the failure of human institutions. He spoke critically of democracy, monarchy, fascism, and Marxism. He was acutely aware of the shortcomings of his own communion, because of his superiors' failure to allow him to publish, teach or lecture. He also knew that in every evolutionary scheme it is difficult for new and improved strains to become dominant over against the huge majority of past strains. However, he had faith in the mechanism which had produced the past strains and was continuing to produce and weed out the new ones. He believed that the mechanism would help the positive strains win out in the end. When applied to institutions, he believed that they, too, were a part of the mechanism and would produce change, even though that change would have a difficult time surviving amidst all of the pressures of nonchange.

METHODS

Methodology should be consistent with and follow from presupposition, but at times it is hard to distinguish the two. However, there is the possibility that various methods could arise from one presupposition, and therefore some distinction needs to be made. Likewise, it is not always true that a scholar follows his presuppositions with appropriate methods. His methodology may be inconsistent with his presuppositions. It is difficult to separate methodology from presuppositions in Teilhard because he did follow his presuppositions closely.

Synthesis of Methods

There is great variety in Teilhard's methodology. Because he believed in the oneness of all reality, he could emphasize one point of reality at one time and at another time relate everything to another point of reality.

A scientist may choose his methodology from his particular scientific discipline. Inasmuch as he is, say a chemist, he will interpret the material he examines in the light of the principles of chemistry. Teilhard was a scientist, more specifically, a geologist and palaeontologist. There were times when he followed strictly the methodology of one of these disciplines, especially in technical papers which he delivered. His interest, however, was not just in examining the evidence from the viewpoint of a palaeontologist or geologist, but also in relating it to the whole scope of history and pre-history, and the past, present and future meaning of all of this. So there were times that he related his system of thought to the whole of philosophy and thereby used the methodology of philosophy. There were other times that he understood his audience to be theologians and applied theological hermeneutics to the subject at hand. Still other writings were addressed to the nonbelieving world where he assumed the role of an apologist and used the methodology of an apologist.

Whatever else Teilhard might have been, he was also a mystic. His mysticism was not of the exaggerated kind of Meister Eckhardt or John Tauler. If theirs could be described as that which fled the natural world to the transcendent Divine, Teilhard's could be described as that which sought the Divine through the natural world.

Teilhard was also a poet. Often the exactness of his scientific methodology was blunted because he was writing scientism in poetry. The poet's adoration of the world's splendor often overcame the scientist's cold, exact measurement of the world. At these times Teilhard was trying to describe not only the externality of what was observable to the senses, but also the "withinness" behind all of the observable.

All of this variety of methodology is disconcerting to anyone who is committed to a single methodology. The scientist may object that what Teilhard has done is not a pure description of what is sensorily observable. Likewise, each discipline will object that Teilhard belongs to some other discipline, not theirs.[3] Teilhard consciously refused to utilize only one methodology. In a way it might be said that he created his own methodology out of a synthesis of all of the other methodologies.

Phenomenology

Teilhard spoke of himself as a phenomenologist. *The Phenomenon of Man* might be thought of as an examination of the data which appears to the untrained man as well as to the natural scientist. The events which brought about the species of man as we know him can be known by the non-scientific. However, there is more to phenomenology than that. Phenomenology deals with more than sense experience. It witnesses to realities beyond sense experience. It says that these metaphysical realities beyond the mere physical must be taken into account when viewing the world. To call these realities psychic is not enough. They may well partake of the psychic as we experience them, but they have their own objective reality beyond our subjective experience. They are reality itself (ontological), not the creations of men—they are discovered not created.

This is all quite consistent with many of Teilhard's themes. He combines this way of viewing the world with the vitalism of Henri Bergson, and uses it to look at every strata of the universe, life, mind, and man.

Dynamic

A very important part of Teilhard's methodology is his dynamic form. It would be hard even to misinterpret any passage in Teilhard as advocating a static view of nature. The overriding principle of all his works, whether he is discussing science, philosophy, or theology, is that things are alive, moving and growing. There is a dynamic principle at work in all things.

It is better to describe his view of reality as *dynamic* rather than *evolutionary*. *Evolutionary* may describe that which is barely dynamic, or may refer only to change without any purposive drive, or to that which has been dynamic in the past but has come to its conclusion (which Teilhard charges has happened to Darwinism). Teilhard's method is dynamic to the fullest degree, because he believes that significant change is still going on, and purpose is working itself out through the whole system of things. Even structure should be understood as both kind and direction of movement taking place within the power of dynamic universe. In Teilhard, there is no static-dynamic dualism where matter is static and history is dynamic. Matter itself is dynamic rather than static.

Dynamic is not only a better term than *evolutionary*, it is also a better term than *dialectical* to describe Teilhard's thought. For one thing *dialectical* has been too closely associated with dialectical materialism. Teilhard believed in developing new realities, but these were not limited to material realities. *Dialectical* usually (although not necessarily) connotes the idea of a rigid movement from one level to another uniformly across all experience. Teilhard's dynamic reality is much more diverse in its movement, although there is finally a coalescence of diverse elements.

Withinness

Teilhard's most unique method, in light of the fact that he represents natural science, is that he seeks withinness behind the external event and phenomenon. For example, he believes that there is not only outward energy which can be measured and which will eventually dissipate as the universe dies down, but there is also inward energy upon which entropy has no effect. Not only are there molecules but there is a bit of consciousness even at the molecular level. Whereas other scientists are interested in what can be measured and observed with sensory mechanism, Teilhard is also interested in finding the inward reality behind that. Interpreters of Teilhard must be aware that Teilhard seeks this withinness or they will not be able to understand him.

Macrocosm

Many times Teilhard reminds his readers that they must take a macroscopic view of things. They must not look at the changes in the past fifty or one hundred years or even in the last few millennia. They must be willing to look at the changes which have happened in the several billion years of the earth's history. He uses his methodology in examining the world for hopeful signs. He is not impatient with war, poverty, famine and disease the way most social scientists have been, but instead looks over the long range of human history and sees man inventing ways to combat each of these and developing the resources to do so. Instead of examining only the horrors of the twentieth century he looks at the whole of man's development over more than one hundred millennia. This may very well be the most difficult methodology for the interpreter of Teilhard. Everyone has been so conditioned to expect immediate miracles and changes that one can hardly speak in terms of what will happen over the next several thousand years. Yet this latter is a fundamental methodological approach of Teilhard.

Synthesis

Synthesis is a key word in Teilhard's methodology. Whether it is knowledge, law, politics, nations or churches, a synthesis of the whole of reality is slowly taking place and will inevitably come about in the future. This is not the splicing together of bits from here and there, but the transformation of various parts into a new whole. Teilhard sees the biologist and the metaphysician dealing with the same problems—reality, truth, events. He sees the theologian and the scientist attempting to explain the same phenomena—the causes of reality and events. Although there are diversities in approaches and fields of study, they are all moving toward a climactic future in which Christ will be all in all.

Success in delineating presuppositions and methodology in Teilhard is elusive. This attempt may very well be questioned because of things which are left out, not included or somewhat parallel. Nevertheless, these are guidelines to the methods of Teilhard.

X. Teilhard's Influence

During the middle of an earthquake is no time to determine the earthquake's damage. Such assessment will take weeks and months following the few moments of the tremor. The same can be said for assessing the influence and value of a theologian or philosopher. The last half of the twentieth century may even be too soon to assess the influence of a nineteenth-century theologian like Schleiermacher, let alone a twentieth-century thinker like Teilhard. Nevertheless, even if such an evaluation must be hedged with many reservations, it is important to make it.

Since Teilhard insists upon planetization and universalism, he would be pleased to know that his influence has been universal. His thought and work have spread geographically, to Europe, the Americas, Asia, and Africa. Teilhard also has had a universal political influence. Unlike most Western scholars, his work has been the center of study in the Soviet Union and among Marxists worldwide. Teilhard's thought also has had a universal religious influence. It has not only been studied by Roman Catholic thinkers but carefully read by theologians of Protestant persuasion. Beyond this he has also been given serious attention by advocates of humanism.

Beyond these generalities, there are several areas where Teilhard's work has exerted more specific influence. These are in the sciences, philosophy and religion.

THE SCIENCES

Although at least one interpreter has said that Teilhard lost his interest in palaeontology very early, he continued his work in that field throughout his life. He made significant contributions to palaeontological knowledge with field trips in the Gobi Desert, the Ordos, Mongolia and the Himalayas. Many technical papers and addresses came out of this research.

As has been true with many palaeontologists, Teilhard developed an interest in anthropology. The history of man is found at the same time that scientists find the earth's history. Artifacts of man and of prehominids point to the antiquity of certain physical characteristics of the earth. On the other hand, the development of various characteristics of the earth's terrain has affected the history and development of man.

Many of Teilhard's articles deal with anthropology, along with palaeontology, biology, religion or philosophy. His magnum opus, *The Phenomenon of Man,* touches all these areas, but the primary thrust of the book is anthropological. Teilhard uses palaeontological background and descriptions and there is a philosophic-religious motif, but the book is basically a study of man's evolution and his destiny.

Teilhard's greatest influence may very well be in the area of anthropology. His study of man broadens the horizon for scientists as well as for philosophers and theologians. He tries to get each group to see that an interpretation of man must cover the broad scope of the millions of years of the universe and not be limited to the advent of written history. More than that, he demonstrates that man must be seen as the apex of all that has happened before. For a full understanding of man, the scientists must not separate their various disciplines, except for just a moment, but must bring them together. Man is the catalyst which transforms the many disciplines into one phenomenon.

Teilhard's influence has also been felt in the area of biology. Though not a biologist by training or experiment, he was a biological theoretician, or perhaps better, a philosopher of biology. For more than a hundred years biology has been completely Darwinian or neo-Darwinian, with the exception of Soviet biology which follows the biologist Lysenko, who was a Lamarckian. Teilhard criticizes Darwinianism because of its "fixity." In the Darwinian scheme of natural selection nothing significantly new could arise. Teilhard does not deny the factor of natural selection but he also believes in acquired characteristics. This is why he has been called a Lamarckian. What this really means is that Teilhard believes that man can shape the evolutionary process. However, the most significant area of Teilhard's influence on biology is the introduction (or reintroduction) of the idea of orthogenesis, that purpose, not blind accident or unguided natural selection, underlies the evolutionary process. Even if the terms *chance* and *natural selection* are correct technically to use for the process, there is a guiding force which is at work in the selective factor. The reintroduction of these ideas by Teilhard has opened the door ever so slightly for their examination and debate among biologists.

Two of the most famous biologists of the twentieth century have expressed appreciation for Teilhard. In his introduction to Teilhard's *The Phenomenon of Man,* Sir Julian Huxley shows how he and Teilhard followed parallel paths in their developing views of the evolutionary process. Certainly Huxley did not agree with all of Teilhard but he found in Teilhard an eloquent spokesman from whom he could learn. Another leading biologist, Theodosius Dobzhansky, professor at the University of California at Davis, has written a large number of articles dealing with the issues Teilhard has raised. While not necessarily committing himself to Teilhard's position, Dobzhansky has written with warm appreciation of Teilhard's efforts. In fact, he has suggested that there is no reason for orthogenesis not to be appropriate in biological science.

It is not possible for one who is a layman in the sciences to make an accurate evaluation of Teilhard's influence on the sciences. With men such as Huxley and Dobzhansky, as well as articles in *Time* magazine, attributing significance to Teilhard's thought, even a layman must conclude that Teilhard has caused a stir among the scientists. Whether his influence will have lasting significance is not possible to determine at this point of time.

PHILOSOPHY

Although philosophy was not Teilhard's major academic pursuit, as a Jesuit he had a thorough grounding in the subject. However, his philosophic influence has not come because he set out to prove or disprove a particular school of philosophy, or even to begin a new school of philosophy. His influence upon philosophy has come from his attempt to integrate the various disciplines into a kind of *Weltanschauung*, a world view. What came out of his work was a new phenomenology of the cosmos which depended upon intuition as well as empiricism.

Gareth Jones explains Teilhard's phenomenology this way:

> In the first place, a phenomenology of the cosmos is neither metaphysics proper, nor is it philosophy proper. This does not mean to say that it has no connection with these disciplines. It has very definite metaphysical and philosophical consequences, although in itself it resolves none of the ultimate questions regarding the cosmos and it says nothing about the purpose or meaning of the world and of man's existence in it.[1]

I can understand why Jones would say that the phenomenology of the cosmos was neither metaphysics nor philosophy proper because, as Teilhard would put it, he did not start out on his quest as a philosopher but as a man. However, Jones is wrong when he says that Teilhard's phenomenology does not resolve the ultimate questions nor say anything about the purpose or meaning of the world. It is precisely at this point that Teilhard moves between the sciences and philosophy. He finds that using only one methodology does not give answers to the ultimate questions nor discover the meaning of the world and man's existence. It is only when he looks at the totality of phenomena that he can see ultimate meaning. It is this insight that leads Wildiers to say:

> Teilhard's phenomenology, then, may be characterized as an endeavour, through the use of scientific expertise, to give as complete as possible expression to the world in its totality and inner orientation.[2]

It is true that Teilhard's phenomenology is descriptive, but the "inner orientation" is as much a part of the reality which needs to be described as the physical universe itself. Within that "inner orientation" is the meaning of man and his universe.

Only the future will be able to tell us if Teilhard has succeeded in his program in such a way that it will influence the course of philosophy. If his program does succeed, philosophy must leave its obsession with analysis, its preoccupation with positivism—that is, with linguistic syntax and the problem of verifiability—and begin to take up the metaphysical task, the discovery of meaning and the inner reality of phenomena. Most of all, if Teilhard succeeds, philosophy must begin to examine the whole of phenomena and experience rather than isolate and analyze very small segments. It is a happy coincidence that philosophy is already beginning to do this, and so there is a more open climate in which Teilhard's works may be read.

An interesting outcome of Teilhard's work has been the stimulation of dialogue between Christians and Marxists. It is hardly an accident that the first Christian-Marxist dialogues were carried on by men strongly influenced by Teilhard. We have noted many affinities between Teilhard and

Marxism in the chapter on "The Social Implications of Teilhard's Thought." Teilhard and Marxists share a faith in man and in man's future. Few other philosophies are as openly utopian as Teilhard's or the Marxists'. A Rumanian journal, *Cronica*, devoted an entire issue to Teilhard. It has been reported that articles about Teilhard as well as his books have appeared in the University of Moscow. One of the most eloquent testimonies to his influence is the works of Roger Garaudy, a prominent Marxist theoretician.[3] It is too early, however, to determine what the final result of this interaction will be, or how much impact Teilhard will have on Marxism. However, the fact that he opens up the possibility of dialogue is influential in itself.

One other area should be mentioned, and that is the Third World movement—philosophies and theologies that are beginning to come from the Third World—Asia, Africa, Latin America. As yet it is almost impossible to measure Teilhard's influence here, though many of the Third World spokesmen are alert theologically. An examination of Rubem Alves's *A Theology of Human Hope*, shows that he quotes Teilhard several times with appreciation.

RELIGION

Teilhard's works have become very influential in the field of theology. This may be because of the lack of any prominent theologians at the present time. Barth, Brunner, and Tillich all have passed from the scene, and Bultmann never developed a full theological system. However whether the prominence of Teilhard is due to the vacuum or whether it is due to his own genius, his works are still prominent in theology.

One particular area influenced by Teilhard is the theology of hope school. The leader of this group is Jürgen Moltmann, who is very familiar with Teilhard's thought. At times Moltmann sounds very much like a Barthian who has been highly influenced by the work of Teilhard. In the theology of hope there is an emphasis on the future as it affects the present. It is an eschatological system which has a strong faith in the triumph of God in the future. These emphases were not Teilhard's alone, but the widespread resurgence of interest in the future shortly after the printing of Teilhard's works would indicate his influence. Apart from dispensational theology, which has always had a theology of the future, no theology before Teilhard has interpreted even Christ's death and resurrection in terms of futurism. And this theme is now shared by the theology of hope movement and Teilhard. Also it is out of the theology of hope movement that much of the impetus has come for the Christian-Marxist dialogue.

Though Teilhard did not begin to be a theologian, theology was a necessary ingredient and by-product of his work. The dynamic of his system has become very appealing in this time when structure is often shattered and old institutional frameworks are left in shambles. Even process theology has become a much stronger movement after the publication of Teilhard's works. It is not that process theology is dependent upon Teilhard, but the dynamism of Teilhard creates a climate in which process theology can grow.

Without a doubt the Roman Catholic church has been influenced by the life and work of Teilhard. He is not the kind of confrontational theologian that Hans Küng has proved to be, but nevertheless he brings about some reexamination, redefinition and restructuring. Philip Hefner reports that "since 1963, for example, of 4,591 indexed articles and books on Jesuit figures, 1,188 deal with Teilhard."[4] Book after book has been written by Roman Catholic scholars extolling Teilhard's work and attempting both to understand and defend him.

Teilhard is not without his opponents within the Roman Catholic church, but these do not detract but merely add to the accounting of his influence. He is important enough that some Catholic scholars have felt it necessary to point out the errors in his work. He is important enough that a papal bull was issued in reaction to his work. This act is generally regarded as a warning to those who would follow Teilhard's evolutionary thought, but some interpreters believe that it was an attempt to set forth the guidelines whereby scholars could participate in the research that Teilhard had begun.

It is understandable that Teilhard would have an influence within his own confessional group, but he also has had an influence on other traditions within Christianity. Numerous books have been written by Protestant authors ranging from conservative to humanistic.

A new brand of mysticism has arisen around Teilhard. The charisma which Teilhard must have had in his person has stretched across the horizon of his death to present-day mystics. The fact that he can be looked upon as something of a martyr who was oppressed by a structured institution has added to that charisma. Also he is seen as a free spirit who dared to think his own thoughts, a view which strikes a familiar chord in many of the present generation. Unfortunately, some devotees of Teilhardianism have failed to recognize Teilhard's personal discipline which accompanied his free spirit.

There have even been songs written and recorded which reflect Teilhard's thought. The best known were written and recorded by Sebastian Temple. His published song booklet is entitled "The Universe Is Singing," with the subtitle "Twelve Songs in the Spirit of Teilhard de Chardin." The first song is entitled, "I Sing a Song of Teilhard."[5] This is certainly not a classical Roman Catholic mysticism but is a kind of twentieth-century personality cult.

Another evidence of Teilhard's influence is the several groups which have organized for the study and promotion of his ideas. In the U.S. there are the American Teilhard de Chardin Association, Inc., and The Phenomenon of Man Project, Incorporated. The Teilhard de Chardin Association of New South Wales is an Australian group. In Italy there are the Centro di Studie di Ricerca Teilhard de Chardin-Instituto Stensen, and the Instituto Ricerche Applicate Documentacione Studi (Irades). A Teilhard study group has been formed in Cape Province in South Africa. There are also over forty study groups meeting in England, Scotland and Ireland.

Whether or not Teilhard's influence is lasting, only the future can tell us (ironically enough). Nevertheless Teilhard's thought has exerted a considerable influence in several disciplines within a decade after his death.

XI. An Assessment of Teilhard's Life Work

Beyond the examination of his influence, what is an appropriate assessment of Teilhard's life and work? His life was apparently marked by serenity and intensity. He was very aggressive in pushing forward his ideas and programs. Yet there was also a serenity in him when he faced the problems and objections which inevitably came. Unlike so many who have found their life's work thwarted, he did not turn to cynicism, but used rejection as a reason to reexamine his thoughts and processes.

He practiced what he preached. He had said that the problem with scientists was that they failed to look at the macrocosm. He wanted them to see man in light of the history of the universe rather than just in light of his pilgrimage since he became an historical being who had learned to write. He felt that only then could one see the proper perspective of the movement of the evolution of man and culture. Teilhard was able to do this in his own life. He saw his rejection by his church not as the end of the world but as one more step toward the world's moving to hyperconsciousness. He believed that his position would sooner or later become a dominant position. He recognized that truth did not begin with the masses but with a few forerunners who saw the future, the road ahead, by their intuitive insight. He believed that he was among those who saw the future. Thereby instead of being angry or cynical about the rejection of his *avant-garde* ideas, he recognized that he fit his own pattern of enunciating history.

Teilhard was an integrated man in the sense that he put together the components (scientist, religionist, etc.) into a whole man. While he would not have wanted to deny being a scientist or a churchman, he would probably have been far more eager to have been a real man rather than any one of these at the exclusion of the other.

A POSITIVE ASSESSMENT

Teilhard's work shows a serious effort to produce an integrated totality. There have been many successful attempts to extend knowledge vertically to the place where a person knows more and more about narrower and narrower fields of study. Certainly there are several areas of Teilhard's work in which he does extend the field of study in this manner. His greatest contribution, however, is probably his attempt to widen the scope of man's knowledge horizontally, by bringing together the many areas of human knowledge and integrating them. For Teilhard, science, religion, economics, or politics are not worlds to themselves but all of these fit together to make up one integrated universe.

For instance, Teilhard integrates history and nature, subjects that have historically been separate. This can be seen most graphically in the division between East and West. Western civilization has emphasized the historical and the Oriental thinkers have emphasized nature. Teilhard balances the two so as to show how the forces of nature affect the historical process and how the historical process in turn intensifies the forces of nature.

Teilhard also does away with the polarity between God and the world. The kind of hostility which religion has often expressed toward the world has no place in Teilhard's thought. He sees the world as the creation of God and the arena in which God works. It is a friendly mechanism and instrument for the purposes of God. He refuses to concentrate on one without the other but considers them together as an integral whole.

In a world which has become so negative and pessimistic, the note of optimism in Teilhard is refreshing. It is not, however, a denial of many horrendous situations which plague the world. Robert Speaight gives an example of Teilhard's attitude.

> Our conversation . . . turned to the atom bomb. Here, surely, was occasion for despair. Teilhard could hardly have foreseen so rapid or catastrophic a conquest of atomic energy; yet the catastrophe was only incidental to the conquest. And so, even in the face of these appalling possibilities, he would hear nothing of despair.[1]

Teilhard admits that there are problems, many of which are serious, but he views these as necessary crises moving the world toward the kind of survival pattern which will develop the future along the lines that are necessary for world fulfillment. This optimism is not based on the past nor upon a naïve view of nature but upon the purposive principles at work whereby the future determines the movement of present events just as it has determined the events of the past.

PROBLEMS IN TEILHARD

Science

Teilhard has always faced opposition from orthodox science. There is an orthodoxy among scientists just as there is an orthodoxy among theologians. Mihaly Czikszentmihalyi says that

> few scientists admit any value to Teilhard's notions, although some outstanding scientists like biologist Julian Huxley and geneticist Theodosius Dobzhansky have not dismissed his

ideas out of hand. Most scientists, however, have followed the lead provided by Peter Medawar, the Nobel Prize winning virologist, whose virulent review of *The Phenomenon of Man* set the tone for an almost general ostracism of the French Jesuit in scientific circles. When about eight years ago I asked one of my genetics teachers in graduate school, the answer was that the man was a charlatan to be forgotten as soon as possible; this I found later to be a fairly typical reaction.[2]

The present orthodox biological methodology is that of laboratory experiments. Teilhard's projections are based upon nonlaboratory work. This has caused many orthodox biologists to reject Teilhard as nonscientific and his program as fantasy.

Peter Medawar, Teilhard's foremost critic, accuses him of building a "system" out of evolution. Bernard Towers, in his interpretative book, *Concerning Teilhard*, responds to Medawar: "The myth that science works through a wholly inductive process of reasoning has long since been exploded by Popper, Braithwaite and Polanyi." [3]

Another serious breach of orthodoxy is Teilhard's Lamarckianism. Lamarck never gained the fancy of the academic world and was not taken seriously after the publication of Darwin's *Origin of Species*. The laboratory biologists have not been able to substantiate Lamarck's theory of acquired characteristics. This does not cause Teilhard to think any less of Lamarckianism. He reasons that a significant step in the changing of a species comes only after an extremely long period of time, and of course that kind of control is not possible in a laboratory situation. The changes also come because they are needed according to the purpose behind the species. They do not come just because of a desired effect.

Orthogenesis is also unorthodox as far as science is concerned. Early Darwinianism assumed the neutrality of nature, so that the survival of the fittest followed along accidental or chance lines. More recent evolutionary theory is more positivistic and rules out a discussion of purpose or nonpurpose but simply examines the biological mechanisms. One must be careful not to write off the biological positivists with the same prejudice and ease with which they write off the metaphysicians. Nevertheless it may be that Teilhard raises the issue of whether science is to stay the captive of the positivists.

Teilhard also differs with a large segment of the scientific community on the nature of evolutionary change. He believes that the changes are significant qualitative leaps rather than small steps on a continuum. James Birx summarizes it:

> Wallace, Fiske, Bergson, Alexander, Smuts and Morgan also held that there were qualitative leaps in evolution and therefore argued that man represents such a leap. As a result, they maintained that man differs in *kind* from the other lower or earlier animals. But Lamarck, Schopenhauer, Spencer, Darwin, Huxley, Nietzsche, Haeckel, Marx, Engels, Lenin, Sellars, and Dewey held that evolution represents a continuum without sudden leaps. They argued that man differs merely in degree from the other primates. The distinction man differing in *kind* or *degree* from the other animals is crucial, as it determines whether man is believed to have a supernatural aspect or to be merely a product of biological evolution respectively.[4]

Teilhard proposes that there are two kinds of energy—tangential and radial. Again this is not orthodox science. Science recognizes physical energy which Teilhard calls tangential or the "withoutness." However, radial energy or "withinness," according to Teilhard, is not subject to laboratory experimentation, and therefore resistance to accepting this second kind of energy can be expected from orthodox scientists.

Teilhard was one of the last persons in the world who would have wanted to deny the advances which have been made by science. He saw that with technology there was coming about the kind of intensification of the noosphere which would be significant in moving the universe toward its final Omega Point. However Teilhard was not intimidated by the scientific world as many theologians have been. He was willing to challenge its basic presuppositions, and to do so without all the laboratory proof in his hand. Therefore, he did not play by the scientists' rules but freely admitted that truth came by intuition as well as by empiricism. Perhaps Teilhard makes it possible for others who are knowledgeable in areas of science and the spirit to have the courage to speak out rather than to stay in subjection to the positivists who have taken over science and have elevated their methodology as the only scientific methodology.

Christian Theology

Teilhard also faces a problem with orthodox Christianity. At best, many of his ideas are incapable of being expressed by orthodox, conventional and traditional dogmas. At worst, many of his ideas are possibly contrary to the dogma of the church and Christianity in general. I use the word *possibly* because there are many who tried to defend Teilhard against the charges of irregularity or heresy. They have tried to demonstrate that Teilhard is saying the same thing as dogma or within the parameters of dogma in another language and from another perspective.

UNIVERSALISM

One of the problems of Teilhard is his apparent universalism. He does admit that if a church says there is a hell that he would agree to that particular dogma. His universalism is one which will appear in the future when the Christosphere and the Omega Point are reached. Then there will come to be a hyperpersonal or a superpersonalized universe in which all people become a part of the structure of mankind which is really the body of Christ. The "withinness" of the human race and the development process of evolution are aiming for this universalism. The process can be speeded up by the work of the church, but it is not a direct product of the institutional church. Therefore this kind of universalism is seen by some interpreters as a threat to orthodox Christianity.

THE DOCTRINE OF GOD

Teilhard's doctrine of God also poses a problem for orthodox Christianity. Nowhere does he deny the historical creedal statements, but his system implies that his idea of God is considerably different from what has been understood by historic Christianity. He tends to see God as being closely involved in the whole process of the developing world—a pantheism of sorts. It is not at all clear, but it might be that what Teilhard talks about is an apotheosis of man, if not of the whole world, when man reaches the Omega Point. Man will then be divine. If this is so, Teilhard's belief is much more like Eastern Christianity (especially Origen) than the orthodoxy which developed in Western Christianity.

REVELATION

There is some question about the orthodoxy of Teilhard's view of revelation. To use Emil Brunner's language, is there any special revelation or is there only general revelation? Teilhard places a great deal of emphasis on the intuitive nature of man, so that the theologian must ask whether or not this replaces the orthodox idea of revelation. His comments on revelation make it appear as though he is talking about a much more natural process than a supernatural event of God.

CREATION

Teilhard raises doubts about whether he agrees with the idea of *creatio ex nihilo*, creation out of nothing, which has been the traditional formula of creation by orthodox Christianity. Does Teilhard really believe in a kind of eternal universe upon which God, who is the inner moving dynamic within the universe, operates and begins to bring order out of the chaos? If so, this sounds much more like an organizing process than it does an original creation out of nothing.

THE PROBLEM OF SIN, EVIL AND ERROR

Teilhard wrote much about the problem of evil, but he never satisfied the representatives of orthodox Christianity. His interpreters have often defended his work against the charge of unorthodoxy at this point. It is the same problem that every Christian theologian faces who admits the reality of sin and evil in a world that is supposed to be in the hands of a beneficent and capable God. It certainly is a heightened problem in Teilhard's work because he sees the movement from dark into light as a part of the program for the universe. The different stages of the world are necessary in order to reach the final stage. The world is not perfect yet, because it must go through various stages in order to arrive at the critical threshold whereby it will be transformed. Teilhard does not see evil as a kind of black specter but as a necessary part of the world's movement toward the ultimate Omega Point.

Gareth Jones comments that for Teilhard,

> evil and sin are simply by-products of evolution. They are peripheral deviations of a natural process, having nothing to do with the central problem of life. . . .
> To him, then, evil is a by-product of evolution. This is because evolution advances by means of groping and chance, with the result that checks and mistakes are always possible. Furthermore, for every one success in evolution there are many failures.[5]

While it may be true that for Teilhard's system evil and sin are simply by-products, for the man who is suffering because of a throw-off of the evolutionary system or from the imperfections of the evolutionary system, the problem of sin and evil (and their accompanying suffering) is hardly a by-product but is a profound question. It may sound good to the particular system to say that suffering is just paying the price of universal progress in triumph and that it is inevitable, but it is hardly satisfactory to the one who is suffering. The only reason this can be accepted as a valid argument for Teilhard is that he was willing to accept his own personal frustration, his physical, mental and spiritual anguish, as being caused by the evolutionary process. Whatever he thought of his own suffering, he saw himself in the middle of the evolutionary stream and not a throw-off of evolution. One cannot help but wonder, however, what Teilhard might have felt had he recognized that he was a by-product of evolution to be cast off as a dead-end street in the world process.

It is not enough to deal with physical evil as a result of evolution, but some accounting must be made of the moral evil which appears as soon as evolution has reached the stage in which there is reflective consciousness and freedom of choice. Inasmuch as man is an imperfect and incomplete being, there is no alternative but that he will use his freedom for evil ends, and his consciousness is not so great but what he fails to think correctly.

While the problem of sin, evil and error is foremost in Teilhard, it does not belong to him alone any more than it does to any other Christian theologian or thinker. There is sin in the world and there is a God who is both beneficent and capable, loving and powerful. Every Christian thinker must account for those three aspects or choose between or redefine them.

Teilhard builds a beautiful system. There may be some real question as to whether the fundamental foundations of the system are true or not. Those who are accustomed to traditional theological language will find it difficult to gain rapport with the work of Teilhard. Only those with a sunny disposition of inordinate optimism who are willing for the most dramatic days to be far in the future will feel comfortable with Teilhard.

Appendix

Chronology of Events in Teilhard's Life

1881	Born, Sarcenat, near Orcines, France	1913	Studied excavations in northern Spain
1892	Entered Jesuit school —Notre Dame de Mongre	1914–19	Stretcher bearer in Moroccan regiment
1892	Received first communion	1919–22	Doctoral studies at Sorbonne
1899	Entered Jesuit noviti- ate	1920–22	Taught at the Institut Catholique in Paris
1900	Entered school at La- val (in his Junior year)	1923–24	In China working out of Tientsin
1901	The school fled to Jer- sey	1924–26	In Paris
1901	Took first vows	1926–27	In Tientsin
1905–8	Went to Cairo to teach	1927–28	In France
1908	Theological studies at Hastings on Sussex	1928	Expeditions in French Somaliland and Ethiopia
1911	Ordination to priest- hood	1929–30	In China
1912	Examined Piltdown man (Eoanthro- pus)	1929	Sinanthropus discov- ered and evaluated
1912–14	Studied science in Paris	1930	Return to Paris and visit to U.S.
		1931	Return to China
		1931–32	Croisière Jaune
		1932	In China working out of Peking

1932–33	Paris visit		Collège de France
1933–35	In China (Peking)		and refused *impri-*
1935	Paris visit		*matur*
1935	Visit India	1948	Visited U.S.
1936	Visit Java	1951	Visited South Africa,
1936–37	In China (Peking)		and toured Buenos
1937	Visit Paris, U.S. and		Aires and Rio de
	Burma		Janeiro on his way
1937–38	In China (Peking)		to New York
1938	Returned to Paris via	1951–55	Lived in U.S.
	Japan and U.S.	1953	Visited South Africa
1939	Visit U.S.		again and returned
1939–46	In China (unable to		via South America
	leave during World	1953	Visited G. G. Simpson
	War II)		in New Mexico, vis-
1946–51	Lived in Paris		ited U. of Califor-
1947	Made an officer in the		nia at Berkeley and
	Legion d'Honneur		Glacier Park
1948	Visited Rome	1954	Last visit to France
1948	Not allowed to accept	1955	Died Easter Sunday,
	professorship at		April 11

Notes

CHAPTER I

1. Morris West, *The Shoes of the Fisherman* (New York: Dell Publishing Co., 1963), pp. 107 f.
2. Ibid., p. 262.
3. Pierre Teilhard de Chardin, *Letters From a Traveller* (New York and Evanston: Harper & Row, 1962), p. 142.
4. Ibid., p. 155.
5. Ibid., p. 178.
6. Pierre Teilhard de Chardin, *How I Believe* (New York: Harper & Row, 1969).
7. Ibid., p. 64.
8. Abbé Paul Grenet, *Teilhard de Chardin, the Man and His Theories* (New York: Paul S. Eriksson, 1966), p. 62.
9. Teilhard de Chardin, *How I Believe*, p. 61.
10. Ibid., pp. 69, 70.
11. Ibid., p. 72
12. Ibid., pp. 74 f.
13. Pierre Teilhard de Chardin, *Building the Earth* (London-Dublin: Geoffrey Chapman, 1965), p. 34, note.
14. Teilhard de Chardin, *How I Believe*, p. 13.
15. See ibid., p. 3.
16. Ibid., p. 30.
17. Ibid., pp. 44–45.
18. Ibid., pp. 27–28.
19. Teilhard de Chardin, *Letters From a Traveller*, p. 160.
20. Claude Cuenot, *Science and Faith in Teilhard de Chardin* (London: Garnstone Press, 1967), p. 22.
21. Pierre Teilhard de Chardin, *Hymn of the Universe* (New York and Evanston: Harper & Row, 1961), p. 23.
22. Ibid., p. 24.

23. Pierre Teilhard de Chardin, *Human Energy* (New York: Harcourt Brace Jovanovich, 1962), pp. 163–81.

CHAPTER II

1. Teilhard de Chardin, *Hymn of the Universe*, pp. 68–70.
2. Pierre Teilhard de Chardin, *The Phenomenon of Man*, 2nd Harper Torchbook edition (New York: Harper & Bros., 1965), p. 64.
3. Ibid., p. 51.

CHAPTER III

1. Henri de Lubac, S.J., *Teilhard de Chardin: The Man and His Meaning* (New York: Hawthorn Books, 1965), pp. 227–38.
2. Piet Smulders, S.J., *The Design of Teilhard de Chardin* (Westminster, Md.: The Newman Press, 1967), pp. 45–59.
3. Pierre Teilhard de Chardin, *Activation of Energy* (New York: Harcourt Brace Jovanovich, 1970), pp. 262–63.
4. Teilhard de Chardin, *The Phenomenon of Man*, pp. 47–48.
5. Ibid., pp. 48–49.
6. Teilhard de Chardin, *Activation of Energy*, p. 56.
7. Ibid.
8. Hans Jonas, *The Phenomenon of Life* (New York: Harper & Row, 1966), p. 25.
9. Teilhard de Chardin, *Hymn of the Universe*, p. 27.
10. Ibid., p. 65.
11. Teilhard de Chardin, *The Phenomenon of Man*, p. 108, and footnote.
12. Ibid., pp. 108–109.
13. Ibid., pp. 71–72.

CHAPTER IV

1. Teilhard de Chardin, *The Phenomenon of Man*, p. 294.
2. Teilhard de Chardin, *Human Energy*, p. 155.
3. Teilhard de Chardin, *The Phenomenon of Man*, pp. 264–67.
4. Teilhard de Chardin, *Human Energy*, pp. 155–60.
5. Ibid., pp. 156 f.
6. Ibid., p. 94.
7. Ibid., p. 95.
8. Ibid., p. 109.
9. Ibid., p. 91.
10. Christopher F. Mooney, S.J., *Teilhard de Chardin and the Mystery of Christ* (Garden City, New York: Image Books, 1968), pp. 78–85.

11. Teilhard de Chardin, *Human Energy*, p. 45.
12. Ibid., p. 46.
13. Teilhard de Chardin, *The Phenomenon of Man*, pp. 292–93.
14. Ibid., pp. 254–72.
15. Ibid., pp. 309–310.
16. Ibid., pp. 262–63.
17. Teilhard de Chardin, *Building the Earth*, p. 62
18. Teilhard de Chardin, *The Phenomenon of Man*, p. 294.

CHAPTER V

1. Teilhard de Chardin, *The Phenomenon of Man*, p. 141.
2. P. G. Fothergill, "Teilhard and the Question of Orthogenesis," in Anthony Dyson and Bernard Towers, eds., *Evolution, Marxism & Christianity* (London: Garnstone Press, 1967), pp. 30–46.
3. Hominisation means the processes and events by which the original human stock became and is still becoming truly human.
4. Teilhard de Chardin, *The Phenomenon of Man*, p. 140
5. Ibid., pp. 120–22.
6. George B. Murray, S.J., "Teilhard and Orthogenetic Evolution," in *Harvard Theological Review* (1967), pp. 281–95.
7. Teilhard de Chardin, *The Phenomenon of Man*, pp. 168–89.
8. Theodosius Dobzhansky, "Teilhard de Chardin and the Orientation of Evolution," *Zygon* 3, No. 3 (Sept. 1968): 242–58.

CHAPTER VI

1. Teilhard de Chardin, *The Phenomenon of Man*, p. 306.
2. Ibid., pp. 41 f.
3. Pierre Teilhard de Chardin, *The Future of Man*, Harper Torchbook edition (New York: Harper & Row, 1969), p. 33.
4. Ibid., p. 118.
5. Teilhard de Chardin, *Activation of Energy*, p. 17.
6. Ibid., p. 225.
7. Ibid.
8. E. C. Rust, *Evolutionary Philosophies and Contemporary Theology* (Philadelphia: The Westminster Press, 1969), p. 75.
9. Kenneth Keniston, *The Uncommitted* (New York: Dell Publishing Co., 1970).
10. Teilhard de Chardin, *The Future of Man*, p. 74.
11. Theodore Roszak, *The Making of a Counter Culture* (New York: Doubleday & Co., 1969), p. 201.
12. Paul Goodman, *Making Do* (New York: New American Library, 1964).
13. Martin Buber, *Paths in Utopia* (Boston: Beacon Press, 1949), p. 14.

14. Teilhard de Chardin, *Activation of Energy*, p. 184.
15. Ibid., p. 18.
16. Teilhard de Chardin, *Building the Earth*, p. 26.
17. Teilhard de Chardin, *The Future of Man*, p. 248.
18. Pierre Teilhard de Chardin, *Letters to Two Friends, 1926–1952* (New York: New American Library, 1968), p. 99.
19. Teilhard de Chardin, *The Future of Man*, pp. 250 f.
20. Ibid., p. 48.
21. Ibid., p. 123.
22. Ibid., p. 202.
23. Teilhard de Chardin, *Building the Earth*, p. 28.
24. Teilhard de Chardin, *Letters From a Traveller*, p. 224.
25. Herbert Marcuse, *Reason and Revolution* (New York: Oxford University Press, 1941), p. 288.

CHAPTER VII

1. Joseph V. Kopp, *Teilhard de Chardin Explained* (Netherlands: The Mercier Press, 1964), p. 51.
2. I have heard individuals related to the Phenomenon of Man Incorporated attribute this position to Teilhard himself. However, I do not recall ever having seen Teilhard put this kind of timetable on the possibility of reaching another threshold.
3. Teilhard de Chardin, *The Phenomenon of Man*, p. 238.
4. Pierre Teilhard de Chardin, *Science and Christ* (New York and Evanston: Harper & Row, Publishers, 1965), pp. 151–73.
5. It is interesting that Paul J. Kelly recently published an article entitled "Empedocles and Teilhard" in the *Teilhard Review* 6 (Winter 1971–72):76–83.
6. Bernard Delfgaauw, *Evolution: The Theory of Teilhard de Chardin* (New York and Evanston: Harper & Row, 1969), pp. 66 f.
7. Teilhard de Chardin, *The Phenomenon of Man*, p. 110.
8. Ibid., pp. 141–46.
9. P. G. Fothergill, "Teilhard and the Question of Orthogenesis," p. 37.
10. Pierre Teilhard de Chardin, *The Vision of the Past* (New York: Harper & Row, 1966), p. 272.
11. Teilhard de Chardin, *The Future of Man*, p. 192.
12. Ibid., p. 65.
13. Ibid., p. 68.
14. Ibid., p. 74.
15. Teilhard de Chardin, *Science and Christ*, p. 164.
16. Ibid.
17. Ibid., p. 170.
18. Teilhard de Chardin, *The Future of Man*, p. 199.
19. Teilhard de Chardin, *Science and Christ*, p. 295.

20. Teilhard de Chardin, *The Phenomenon of Man*, p. 264.
21. Mooney, *Teilhard de Chardin and the Mystery of Christ*, p. 165.
22. Teilhard de Chardin, *The Phenomenon of Man*, p. 183.
23. For a detailed discussion of this see Teilhard's *The Phenomenon of Man*, the chapter entitled "The Deployment of the Noosphere," pp. 190–211.
24. Teilhard gives a long discussion of the noosphere and its development in his book *Man's Place in Nature*, pp. 79–123.
25. Teilhard de Chardin, *The Future of Man*, p. 169.
26. Ibid., p. 177.
27. Teilhard de Chardin, *The Phenomenon of Man*, p. 255.
28. Ibid., pp. 268–72.
29. Ibid., p. 270.
30. Teilhard de Chardin, *Science and Christ*, p. 165.
31. N. M. Wildiers, *An Introduction to Teilhard de Chardin* (New York: Harper & Row, 1968), p. 138.
32. Teilhard de Chardin, *Science and Christ*, p. 164.
33. Teilhard de Chardin, *How I Believe*, p. 82.
34. Wildiers, *An Introduction to Teilhard de Chardin*, p. 139.
35. Teilhard de Chardin, *Science and Christ*, p. 14.
36. Teilhard de Chardin, *How I Believe*, p. 82.
37. Mooney, *Teilhard de Chardin and the Mystery of Christ*, pp. 165 f.
38. Teilhard de Chardin, *How I Believe*, see Chapter 3, "The Universal Christ and the Convergence of Religions," pp. 77–85.
39. Kopp, *Teilhard de Chardin Explained*, p. 59.
40. Ibid., pp. 56 f.
41. Wildiers, *An Introduction to Teilhard de Chardin*, p. 91.

CHAPTER VIII

1. Pierre Teilhard de Chardin, *Letters to Leontine Zanta* (New York: Harper & Row, 1969), p. 29.
2. Pierre Teilhard de Chardin, *The Making of a Mind* (London: Collins, 1965), pp. 66 f.
3. Robert Speaight, "Teilhard de Chardin the Man," *Teilhard de Chardin: Re-Mythologization* (Waco, Texas: Word Books, 1970), p. 133.
4. Teilhard de Chardin, *Letters to Leontine Zanta*, p. 30.
5. Teilhard de Chardin, *How I Believe*, p. 16.
6. Cuenot, *Science and Faith in Teilhard de Chardin*, p. 17.
7. Teilhard de Chardin, *Letters to Leontine Zanta*, p. 29.
8. Grenet, *Teilhard de Chardin: The Man and His Theories*, p. 57.
9. Ibid., pp. 76–77.
10. Cuenot, *Science and Faith in Teilhard de Chardin*.

CHAPTER IX

1. Teilhard de Chardin, *How I Believe,* p. 3.
2. Donald P. Gray, *The One and the Many* (New York: Herder and Herder, 1969), p. 11.
3. My first introduction to Teilhard was by a professor teaching philosophy who spoke of Teilhard being more of a scientist than a philosopher. Later the head of a biology department at a state university lectured on Teilhard at a meeting I attended and spoke of Teilhard as being more of a theologian. Theologians and clergymen who have studied Teilhard have spoken of him as being gifted in other fields but that his interest was not in technical religion.

CHAPTER X

1. D. Gareth Jones, *Teilhard de Chardin: An Analysis and Assessment* (Grand Rapids, Michigan: William B. Eerdmans, 1969), p. 29.
2. Wildiers, *An Introduction to Teilhard de Chardin,* p. 50.
3. Mr. Garaudy has recently been removed from leadership in the French Communist Party. This may very well have been a reaction to Garaudy's participation in the Christian-Marxist dialogues.
4. Philip Hefner, *The Promise of Teilhard* (Philadelphia and New York: J. B. Lippincott Company, 1970), p. 14.
5. Sebastian Temple, *The Universe Is Singing* (Chicago: Ephraim Publications).

CHAPTER XI

1. Speaight, "Teilhard de Chardin the Man," p. 13.
2. Mihaly Czikszentmihalyi, "Sociological Implications in the Thought of Teilhard de Chardin", *Zygon* 5 (June 1970) :130.
3. Bernard Towers, *Concerning Teilhard* (London: Collins, 1969), p. 91.
4. H. James Birx, *Pierre Teilhard de Chardin's Philosophy of Evolution* (Springfield, Ill.: Charles C. Thomas Publishers, 1972), p. 82.
5. Jones, *Teilhard de Chardin: An Analysis and Assessment,* p. 57.

Glossary

ANTHROPOGENESIS. The development of man as a purely physical being, taken as a whole.

BIOGENESIS. The rise and development of life.

BIOSPHERE. The realm, envelope or layer of living things which now forms a covering over the earth.

CENTREISM (CENTRATION). The principle and process of the intensification and interiorization of all reality which continues to increase throughout the evolutionary process.

CHRISTOGENESIS. The term coined by Teilhard to describe the final phase of evolution (after cosmogenesis, biogenesis, anthropogenesis). This stage is the great synthesis of mankind into the "mystical body of Christ."

COMPLEXITY-CONSCIOUSNESS. A fundamental law according to Teilhard, which correlates psychic energy and reflection with the complexity and concentration of matter. This he believes can be traced from where it was at a minimum in the prehominid world to the development at the present.

CREATIO EX NIHILO. Creation out of nothing. It is the orthodox Christian doctrine that God created the world without benefit of prior substance.

COSMOGENESIS. The development of the universe in accordance with its evolutionary goal.

ÉLAN VITAL. The term used by Henri Bergson to denote the source of inner dynamic of the process of evolution.

ENTROPY. The measure of the gradual dissipation (or unavailability) of physical energy which happens in a closed thermodynamic system. It is defined by the Second Law of Thermodynamics.

HOMINISATION. The process and events which aimed toward and culminated in the appearance of man and continues to develop and realize the potential within man.

LAMARCKIANISM. The theory of evolution that environmental changes caused structural changes in life forms.

METAPHYSICS. The division of philosophy that studies the science of being, causes, cosmology and ontology.

NOOGENESIS. The birth and development of reflective thought.

NOOSPHERE. The stage of evolution where there is an envelope or realm of thought embracing reality but still dependent on previous realms (biosphere, cosmos).

OMEGA POINT. The climax of evolution where there is the convergence of the material and spiritual. It is often identified by Teilhard with the Second Coming of Christ.

ONTOLOGY. The science of being and reality. It investigates the nature and essence of being.

ORTHOGENESIS. The theory that variations in successive generations is the result of (or influenced by) an inner mechanism rather than the result of natural selection only.

PALAEONTOLOGY. The science that deals with the study of past geological periods.

PANENTHEISM. The belief that all is encompassed in God or that all is the property of God.

PANTHEISM. The belief that reality and God are coextensive with one another and that there is nothing of either outside of the other.

PEDUNCLE. The stalk, or stem, or beginning bud of a new phylum.

PHENOMENOLOGY. It commonly refers to a scientific description of actual phenomena which purports to be a nonphilosophical enterprise. Philosophically it can be a descriptive analysis of a subjective process or the study of universals and essences which are nonindividual objects but which present themselves directly to the consciousness. Apparently, Teilhard used the term in its scientific and philosophical senses.

PLANETIZATION. The belief that man will finally completely encompass the earth, that mankind will then enclose upon itself and form a single entity.

RADIAL ENERGY. The inner "psychic" energy which causes centreism and increasing complexity.

TANGENTIAL ENERGY. The external energy which governs external relations of like elements.

TRANSFORMISM. The theory that species are changed into new species through modifications in successive generations.

Bibliography

BOOKS BY TEILHARD DE CHARDIN

Activation of Energy. New York: Harcourt Brace Jovanovich, Inc., 1970.

The Appearance of Man. New York: Harper & Row, Publishers, 1965.

Building the Earth. London-Dublin: Geoffrey Chapman, 1965.

The Divine Milieu. New York: Harper & Row, Publishers, 1960.

The Future of Man. New York: Harper & Row, Publishers, 1964.

How I Believe. New York: Harper & Row, Publishers, 1969.

Human Energy. New York: Harcourt Brace Jovanovich, Inc., 1962.

Hymn of the Universe. New York: Harper & Row, Publishers, 1961.

Letters from a Traveller. New York: Harper & Row, Publishers, 1962.

Letters to Leontine Zanta. New York: Harper & Row, Publishers, 1969.

Letters to Two Friends, 1926–1952. New York: The New American Library, Inc., 1968.

The Making of a Mind. St. James' Place, London: Collins, 1965.

Man's Place in Nature. London: Collins, 1966.

The Phenomenon of Man. New York: Harper & Bros. Publishers, 1959.

Science and Christ. New York: Harper & Row, Publishers, 1965.

The Vision of the Past. New York: Harper & Row, Publishers, 1966.

BOOKS ABOUT TEILHARD DE CHARDIN

Birx, H. James. *Pierre Teilhard de Chardin's Philosophy of Evolution.* Springfield, Illinois: Charles C. Thomas Publishers, 1972.

Braybrooke, Neville. *Teilhard de Chardin: Pilgrim of the Future.* London: Darton, Longman & Todd, Ltd., 1964.

Buber, Martin. *Paths in Utopia.* Boston: Beacon Press, 1949.

Cuenot, Claude. *Science and Faith in Teilhard de Chardin.* London: Garnstone Press, 1967; New York: Humanities Press, 1967.

Delfgaauw, Bernard. *Evolution: The Theory of Teilhard de Chardin.* New York and Evanston: Harper & Row Publishers, 1969.

de Lubac, Henri, S. J. *Teilhard de Chardin—The Man and His Meaning.* New York: Hawthorn Books, Inc., Publishers, 1965.

———. *The Religion of Teilhard de Chardin.* Image Books ed. Garden City, New York: Doubleday & Company, Inc., 1968.

Dyson, Anthony and Towers, Bernard, eds., *Evolution, Marxism & Christianity.* London: Garnstone Press, 1967.

Goodman, Paul. *Making Do.* New York: The New American Library, Inc., 1964.

Gray, Donald P. *The One and the Many.* New York, New York: Herder and Herder, 1969.

Grenet, Abbé Paul. *Teilhard de Chardin—The Man and His Theories.* New York: Paul S. Eriksson, Inc., 1966.

Hefner, Philip. *The Promise of Teilhard.* Philadelphia and New York: J. B. Lippincott Company, 1970.

Jonas, Hans. *The Phenomenon of Life.* New York: Harper & Row, Publishers, 1961.

Jones, D. Gareth. *Teilhard de Chardin: An Analysis and Assessment,* Grand Rapids, Michigan: William B. Eerdmans Publishing Company, 1969.

Kenniston, Kenneth. *The Uncommitted.* New York: Dell Publishing Co., Inc., 1970.

Kopp, Joseph V. *Teilhard de Chardin Explained.* Netherlands: The Mercier Press, 1964.

Marcuse, Herbert. *Reason and Revolution.* New York: Oxford University Press, 1941.

Mooney, Christopher F., S. J. *Teilhard de Chardin and the Mystery of Christ.* Garden City, New York: Image Books, 1968.

Roszak, Theodore. *The Making of a Counter Culture.* New York: Doubleday & Company, Inc., 1969.

Rust, E. C. *Evolutionary Philosophies and Contemporary Theology.* Philadelphia: The Westminster Press, 1969.

———. *Positive Religion in a Revolutionary Time.* Philadelphia: The Westminster Press, 1970.

———. *Science and Faith.* New York: Oxford University Press, 1967.

Smulders, Piet, S. J. *The Design of Teilhard de Chardin.* Westminster, Maryland: The Newman Press, 1967.

Speaight, Robert; Casserly, J. V. Langmead; and Wilshire, Robert V. *Teilhard de Chardin: Re-Mythologization.* Waco, Texas: Word Books, Publisher, 1970.

Sproxton, Vernon. *Teilhard de Chardin.* London: SCM Press Ltd., 1971.

Temple, Sebastian. *The Universe Is Singing.* Chicago: Ephraim Publications (B.M.I.), 1969.

Tillich, Paul. *Political Expectations.* New York: Harper & Row, Publishers, 1971.

Towers, Bernard. *Concerning Teilhard.* London: Collins, 1969.

West, Morris. *The Shoes of the Fisherman.* New York: Dell Publishing Co., Inc., 1963.

Wildiers, N. M. *An Introduction to Teilhard de Chardin.* New York Harper & Row, Publishers, 1968.

SELECTED ARTICLES ON TEILHARD

Barbour, I. G. "Five Ways of Reading Teilhard (Phenomenon of Man)," *Soundings* 51 (1968):115–45.

———. "The Significance of Teilhard," *Christian Century,* August 1967.

Czikszentmihalyi, Mihaly. "Sociological Implications in the Thought of Teilhard de Chardin," *Zygon* 5 (June 1970):130–47.

Dobzhansky, Theodosius. "Teilhard de Chardin and the Orientation of Evolution," *Zygon* 3 (Summer 1968):242–58.

Kelly, Paul J. "Empedocles and Teilhard," *Teilhard Review* 6 (Winter 1971–72):

Mooney, C. F. "Teilhard de Chardin and the Christological Problem," *Harvard Theological Review* 58 (January 1965):91–126.

Murray, G. B. "Teilhard and Orthogenetic Evolution," *Harvard Theological Review* 60 (July 1967):281–95.